Love Yourself...
And It Doesn't Matter
Who You Marry

For Wölf and Annalena

For Ruth and Eberhard

Love Yourself...
And It Doesn't Matter
Who You Marry

Eva-Maria Zurhorst

Translated by Annette Charpentier

HAY HOUSE

Australia • Canada • Hong Kong
South Africa • United Kingdom • United States

First published and distributed in the United Kingdom by:
Hay House UK Ltd, 292B Kensal Rd, London W10 5BE. Tel.: (44) 20 8962 1230; Fax: (44) 20 8962 1239. www.hayhouse.co.uk

Published and distributed in the United States of America by:
Hay House, Inc., PO Box 5100, Carlsbad, CA 92018-5100. Tel.: (1) 760 431 7695 or (800) 654 5126; Fax: (1) 760 431 6948 or (800) 650 5115. www.hayhouse.com

Published and distributed in Australia by:
Hay House Australia Ltd, 18/36 Ralph St, Alexandria NSW 2015. Tel.: (61) 2 9669 4299; Fax: (61) 2 9669 4144. www.hayhouse.com.au

Published and distributed in the Republic of South Africa by:
Hay House SA (Pty), Ltd, PO Box 990, Witkoppen 2068. Tel./Fax: (27) 11 706 6612. orders@psdprom.co.za

Published and distributed in India by:
Hay House Publishers India, Muskaan Complex, Plot No.3, B-2, Vasant Kunj, New Delhi - 110 070. Tel.: (91) 11 41761620; Fax: (91) 11 41761630. contact@hayhouseindia.co.in

Distributed in Canada by:
Raincoast, 9050 Shaughnessy St, Vancouver, BC V6P 6E5. Tel.: (1) 604 323 7100; Fax: (1) 604 323 2600

A catalogue record for this book is available from the British Library.

Previously published as *Liebe dich selbst und es ist egal, wer du heiratest* by Wilhelm Goldmann Verlag, München, 2004, ISBN 3-442-33722-4

ISBN 978-1-4019-1527-8

Composition by Scribe Design Ltd, Ashford, Kent.
Printed and bound in Great Britain by TJ International, Padstow, Cornwall.

CONTENTS

I didn't love her
because we were well suited.
I just loved her.

Robert Redford as Tom Booker in *The Horse Whisperer*

PREFACE
Don't give up

I know that it can work out. I know that your relationship can be just what you want it to be. Why? Because fate has placed this book in your hands. Maybe it was a present from a well-meaning friend. Maybe somebody said to you, 'Look, if you want to save your relationship, why don't you at least read a book about it?' Maybe your partner threw it at you, shouting, 'Why don't you do something about our relationship, then?' Maybe it simply turned up in front of you – in a bookshop, on a coffee-table or a bedside unit – and said, 'Read me.' Maybe you've been searching for answers for a long time, looking for a new angle, a fundamental change in your relationship... But however you've come to be reading these lines right now, you can be absolutely sure that, consciously or unconsciously, you really want to make your relationship better – or to finally find a meaningful one. You can also be sure that your heart and soul will be committed to this aim, even though your mind may be saying something different.

Where are you now? Have you given up all hope of your relationship ever being deeper and more fulfilling? Have you despaired of ever working things out with your partner? Are you having one affair after the other? Is your partner? Has your sex life lost its sparkle? Is arguing all you ever do? Does your life seem empty or is it just ticking over while you and your partner make small talk?

Maybe you can't forgive each other and are trapped in resentment. Maybe you are waging guerrilla warfare about the toothpaste tube being left open or crumbs being on the table. Maybe things are escalating and it's scaring you. Maybe you have already read dozens of books and been to couple counselling and can still see no solution to your relationship problems.

Don't despair – things can still work out! You and your partner can find the way to each other's heart again – or discover it for the first time. I know that it's possible, even though it might sound like a miracle. When you experience it, it certainly feels like one! And it is within your power. You can have the relationship you want with the partner you have right now – no matter how distant, unattractive or downright disgusting they might seem to you now. I know that it can work out because I have experienced it myself.

I may seem like a specialist in relationships because I have studied the subject for years, have read a lot about it and have learned a lot from wonderfully competent teachers. I have also worked with many people on healing their relationships. That is all very important, but the truth is that I know that things can work out because I am still married to my husband and am deeply grateful for it.

In the beginning we certainly didn't look a dream match. There were years when nobody would have put money on our marriage lasting. Today I believe that forced me to search for the true power in a working relationship. Today I am convinced that life brought us together and threw so many obstacles in our way because our real task was to tackle them, learn self-belief and experience the healing it triggered. Without those challenges we would never have discovered how much love, patience, strength and courage were locked in our hearts. We would never have discovered that two people can overcome seemingly insurmountable difficulties together. And I personally could not have come to accept myself. I couldn't have written this book.

'I know that it can work out!' is the true basis of my work – and of the power within this book.

It is for my daughter and my husband, with deepest gratitude.

Eva-Maria Zurhorst
Wuppertal, June 2003

FOREWORD
English is the language of my soul

Liebe Dich selbst – in English?! What you as a reader will take for granted is very special for me. After this book became a huge overnight success in my native country, just by word of mouth, and was hailed as the ultimate book on relationships, it was translated into many different languages. But English... I got goose-pimples when I read my own words in English for the first time! I also felt deeply grateful.

Over the course of my life English has become the mother tongue of my soul. It started off as a pure coincidence – the first book that gave me a glimpse of my inner world was written in English. A friend of mine gave it to me, but I did not want to read it. For one thing, I found it too difficult. Apart from that, I thought it was probably irrelevant psycho-babble. But the book kept lying around and often seemed to say, 'Hello! Read me!' Eventually my resistance lessened and I actually started reading it.

Not knowing the English language very well, I understood very little rationally. But in a strange way the book's message went straight in at a deeper level. While I was reading it, something opened up in my heart; it made me see the world through totally different eyes. All of a sudden I realized why I was the way I was. All of a sudden I could feel that there was so much more inside me than my eyes could see and my mind could grasp. Later on, I experienced many more such coincidences: people, books, tapes and CDs found their way to me via complicated routes. All of them were in English. All of them had a healing effect on my emotional life. All of them gave me consistent guidance, until one day I realized that the word 'soul' was much more familiar to me than *Seele* in my mother tongue. Sometimes it was like living in a parallel world that I was not able to share easily with others. Ultimately, I felt an ever-stronger need to communicate in my own words everything I had learned in this other language. While I was writing this book I sometimes hoped I would be able to give something back to the English-speaking world which had for so long been a teacher of my soul. I am infinitely grateful to have received this opportunity now.

My thanks go to Michelle Pilley, publisher at Hay House, who shared my belief in this project from our first meeting and who to this day is promoting it in a very personal and warm-hearted way.

And to Dr Chuck Spezzano, my first great (English-speaking) teacher in relationships, who can read now how much my life has been changed by his *Psychology of Vision*. At our first meeting, a few boxes of Kleenex nearly prevented me from even listening to him.

It was at the worst point of my marital crisis that I came across a small leaflet announcing that the 'author of many books and a renowned relationship specialist' was holding a workshop in Germany. At that point I had nothing to lose and I thought, 'A doctor who has written many books on the subject probably has a lot to say. Maybe this is your last chance to save your marriage.'

I went to the workshop secretly, on my own, and after the first few minutes I was thinking, 'Good God, what am I doing here?' There was a box of tissues by every chair and the relationship specialist at the front looked like an evangelical preacher. Everything inside me was urging me to run away. 'No, I'll never cry in front of all these people,' I thought. 'After the break, at the latest, I'll be out of here!'

To cut a long story short, I stayed until the very end and kept having to grab tissues out of the box. It was as if the guy up there was talking about my very own dismal marriage. As if he had heard every single one of my hopeless thoughts. And as if he was absolutely certain that he knew a way out of this mess. He opened my eyes to a completely new way of looking at my relationship. When I came home, I no longer saw the wrong husband and a hopeless marriage doomed to failure, but a great opportunity to finally heal all my old wounds.

I have described the effects of this first encounter in this book. And I still consider it the greatest gift I have ever received. How much love, trust and intimacy have developed between my husband and me since then.

Years later, when my husband and I had not only left our major crisis behind but were moving forward together, we met Jeff and Sue Allen and learned about their work on relationships. In our first workshop with them Jeff told us the story of his own marriage, which over the years I have retold to countless clients of mine in order to clarify what is so often misunderstood: I do not advocate clinging to your current partner at all costs, but letting go in order to finally forge a true relationship.

Jeff and Sue's story illustrates this paradox particularly clearly. Those two had come to a point I was familiar with in my own marriage: a totally bleak outlook with divorce apparently the only option after years of living parallel lives. Jeff, a dedicated mariner, was away somewhere in the Gulf as the captain of a large vessel. He was a kind of Lonesome Cowboy who didn't like 'all that relationship stuff'. Until one morning he woke up on his ship and realized that his hard shell had a crack in it. He was flooded by insecurity. The strong and independent captain collapsed like a punctured tyre. Feelings were surging to the surface that Jeff had kept hidden from the world – and from himself – for a long time.

When he tried to get in touch with his wife at home – whom he had kept at bay emotionally for a long time – he found a strange coincidence had taken place. His front as the strong and independent husband had collapsed at exactly the moment that his wife at home finally had found the courage to let him go.

Sue had always been the dependent one, the needy one in the relationship. She had always been on at Jeff to come home, to be a reliable partner and father. But the more she had pushed him, the sooner he was off again on a ship to the other end of the world. Finally, years of hopelessness had led to something shifting inside Sue and she had found the courage to let go and focus on her own life. It made no sense to be angry and demanding any longer. She decided not to worry any more about what would happen to the children without their father. All of a sudden she felt liberated and ready for the first steps on her own.

Then the telephone rang. It was Jeff, 3,000 miles away on his ship in the Gulf. He said, 'I know. I could feel that you had left.' But that wasn't all. He had resigned from his job and was already on his way home.

With my husband and me, the turnaround was not as dramatic as with Jeff and Sue. But basically we had experienced exactly the same thing. Only when I had found the courage to let go of my husband and the familiar but empty security, only when I had stopped my nagging and whingeing and said with deep conviction, 'We will have to separate' – only then did a space open up in which my husband could slowly move towards me again.

And that is the point I would like to make with this book. It is about the path towards yourself. It is about healing your own wounds. It is about trusting that you can face all your fears and anxieties. Only then does the neediness stop, the clinging, the nagging, the running away, the cutting off, the shutting out. Only then can love arise and unfold – all on its own, without even any grace.

Jeff says about this turning point in his life:

> *I realized this was an important point in my life: I could either go on living a seemingly safe and independent life and distance myself from everyone who meant anything to me, or I could return and have the courage to admit to myself how hungry for love and affection I really was. I could return and dare to take my place as a hurting, dependent partner in an honest relationship.*
>
> *I chose to return to the UK and begged Susie to take me back. Luckily, she refused! I spent four months living on my own, in what could only be described as a pitiful state, but it gave me the heaven-sent opportunity to deal with much of my repressive childhood and the emotions involved. I could at least move forward to the point where I could offer the potential of being a partner willing to learn.*

Thank you, Jeff, for not hiding behind the front of a relationship expert at our first meeting but showing yourself as a human being willing to help because you knew our pain. Thank you, Jeff and Sue, for showing me and confirming to me how hearts and relationships can heal – and how much a couple can give to other people when they not only choose this path themselves but also share it with others.

Wuppertal, December 2006

INTRODUCTION

Leave – so that you can come back

I didn't *want* to write this book. I wrote it because I had to. It wouldn't leave me alone, it gave me no peace and confronted me at every turn. It wanted to be written, and apparently by me.

All my life I have been exploring relationships, even though it took me a long time to realize it. In the past I had all sorts of goals, plans and dreams, but very often, even when I was pursuing them with all my heart, things didn't turn out the way I wanted. Life taught me very early on that I couldn't control it. Instead, it just unfolded, and I was invited to be there.

Life has also taught me, against my will, that it is in constant change – one cycle after another – and that those changes are the true meaning of my life. It has taught me that in each and every one of those cycles some things are finished and die, and through this I am led to rearrange things, to re-evaluate matters and to develop further.

Once these cycles unnerved and frightened me, but gradually I learned to trust that something new would always come out of them. I learned to stay alert, to keep a sense of direction and to hold on to the meaning of my life. I learned to give up familiar patterns and habits which were holding me back. I learned to trust that the unknown path ahead of me might be the best part of the journey and that at the next crossroads another chance of happiness would be waiting for me. Nothing ever really ended.

And every time I resisted this process, the very resistance in me, the fault-line, the presumed blockage, turned out to be a signpost. Every time there was another opportunity to experience a deeper and more authentic feeling of fulfilment than ever before. Time and again I was forced to endure a familiar space becoming empty – only to make room for something new. But all of those apparently new aspects of my life had the same message. Fundamentally my life was always about exploring relationships and accepting myself – even though I was not aware of it for a long time.

When I was five I often felt lonely. Sometimes I was overcome by such a strange fear that I didn't dare mention it to anyone – I had the feeling that life somehow wasn't real. I watched other people and asked myself whether they were all in the know and it was only me that didn't have a clue. I wondered whether the people around me were just actors who had agreed to perform a play and I was the only one who thought everything was real – the only one who experienced *real* fear or who could be *really* happy. Sometimes I asked myself whether it was the other way round – whether I was the only one who thought that something wasn't real about this life and that this was the reason why I often felt lonely and strange while everybody else seemed happy and content.

At school I often had migraine attacks when I was with other people and had to withdraw to a darkened room. During adolescence, when I was in a crowd I would suddenly begin to hyperventilate until I fainted. At 18 I more or less fled my small home town and the Catholic Church in the hope of finding a sense of belonging and faith somewhere else.

In my early twenties I was offered the chance to work in Egypt as a journalist. It was strikingly different from the life I had led so far, on a cultural, religious and geographical level, and this piqued my curiosity. I was fascinated by the all-pervading presence of religion in everyday life. Life and faith seemed closely interlocked, but the price was high. While the muezzins' chants haunted the streets of Cairo, everywhere I went I saw men with frighteningly greedy eyes and women who had given up on themselves.

By the end of my twenties my inner search had taken me as far as the Cape of Good Hope. But even in the land of black and white I couldn't find clarity. Instead I became a tightrope walker between two worlds. I met people who were enemies to the core and yet had the same deep longings – irrespective of the colour of their skin.

At one point I wasn't able to work out my own views on apartheid any more and didn't feel able to carry on working as a journalist. Doing three-minute radio reports on the situation in South Africa seemed like raping the truth. The questions I raised in talks with radical right-wing Boers sporting the swastika or with black guerrilla fighters who had been tortured became less and less political and more and more psychologically oriented. I also talked to blind people about South Africa. They had learned to either smell or hear a different skin colour. To me all this was absurd. I only had one dream – I wanted to bring people of different colours together. To remain true to myself I ended my career as a journalist in South Africa and wrote a book to explore my complex and sometimes confusing encounters with black and white people on the Cape of Good Hope.

Back in Germany, my next apprenticeship in life was already waiting for me. The Berlin Wall had come down. I took a post in communications and later in personnel in a large former East German company in Berlin. After three years of working as a kind of pioneer for the restructuring of the East, I suffered a nervous breakdown on the day I was supposed to present our communication strategies to a larger audience.

The breakdown was only the culmination of a very slow process. For days everything inside me had been resisting giving the presentation. I had written the speech with the greatest of care, as you have to for presentations like that, providing diagrams, facts, figures and business jargon. But none of that had been motivating my work for a long time. Again it was all about people.

This time the contrast was not between blacks and whites. As I was also responsible for the internal communication of the company I had become a kind of interpreter between East and West, between management and workforce. I had held coaching workshops and seminars on personality development and had often been asked by our director to mediate all kinds of negotiations. Again I was being challenged to bridge unmanageable distances between people via communication. Officially I was responsible for my employees and for the day-to-day running of my department. Deep inside I was once more driven by curiosity and the desire to bring people of different backgrounds together.

This time round I tried to meet those demands for a long time. Having a lot of energy, I scheduled myself 12-hour days and a packed diary of events. But I was chain-smoking my way through them and more and more often I was troubled by vague anxiety and a heart arrhythmia for which doctors couldn't find a medical reason. It was as though I was playing a role which I could not let go of any more.

The nervous breakdown had enough impact to get me away from everything and allow me to recover my courage and trust in myself. Without knowing what I was going to do next, I resigned from my very well-paid job. That also meant saying goodbye to the sports car, fashionable penthouse flat, exotic trips and luxury hotels. I renovated a rundown old house and started living a quiet life, earning a living by doing small writing jobs for advertising agencies. I had no idea what the future would hold.

I was burnt out. I felt that I had searched all over the world for answers that did not exist. I was just 32, I had ended a rather erratic career with a nervous breakdown and was now living as a hermit after years of travelling the world. My quest was now reduced to two questions: How could I find fulfilment and do meaningful work at the same time? And how could I create better links between people?

I found a strange answer to those questions: I became pregnant. My intra-uterine coil had become displaced and fate gave me a child with enough desire for life to squeeze past the contraceptive device. And for a father, fate brought me a young man who knew neither doubt nor uncertainty and whose life experience and perspectives could hardly have been more different from mine. He was six years younger than me and used to life giving him everything he wanted without much trouble. He was youthful and attractive, nearly always in a good mood, and he simply wanted to have fun, increase the turnover of his company and enjoy business success. He wanted to do better than his older brothers one day – that was all he expected from life.

Until we met he was mostly engaged in enjoying a hectic social whirl and string of shallow affairs. I felt like a stranger in his world, and not only because I looked very different from the long-legged, lithe creatures he had surrounded himself with before he had met me. He didn't embody any of my ideals either. I felt comfortable in his presence and he made me laugh, but neither of us was smitten at first. Nor was he the creative genius I had dreamed of – neither a gifted architect nor a famous wordsmith. He didn't offer a shoulder to lean on and was searching neither for the meaning of life nor for a woman for life.

Up to this point I had always been on the lookout for a serious relationship, but in vain. Eternally hopeful, I had been in two long-term relationships and had had a series of flings. However, my heart had never felt at rest. I would have loved to have stayed in a relationship, to have given myself totally to another person, but I felt always torn away again. It was either the fear of being abandoned or the fear of being chained. Everybody who knew me was convinced that relationships and me just didn't go together!

My new fiancé and I weren't a spectacular couple. It was hardly the ultimate romance. In fact I barely knew him. We weren't a dream match – everybody could see that. But we were soon to be parents – and it wasn't long before everybody could see that as well. It was clear to me that I was going to have this child. And he was equally clear about it. 'We'll manage!' he said. We left everything behind, moved to a different town and got married.

Two years later: Our daughter is taking her first steps. Our marriage is a middle-class valley of boredom. Mummy cooks the meals, Daddy goes to work. There's no real connection between us. My husband comes home later and later and less often. I feel chained to the sandpit and the playgroup. We argue more and more. Our friends say they knew it would never work out.

Nothing is right, but somehow we don't separate. We put up with it. We settle into habits, routines. We look after our child. In the beginning we muddle through, feeling emotionally and physically numb. Silences follow noisy battles for power. Then there's a torturous cease-fire: comfortable day-to-day existence, secret affairs, career moves, house moves, hopelessness and new beginnings. Still we don't split up. Every time we get to that point we are gripped by sadness and the sudden certainty of a deep inner bond. It's nothing passionate, nothing raw, rather a quiet melancholic memory of our love, and it disappears just as quickly as it arrives.

This feeling is not the answer to my inner search but it has a magical and magnetic power over me. It is like a secret code which I need to break. We both start actively looking for this feeling. We start to explore it. Somehow I begin to sense that a relationship is about something completely different from finding the right person. Something inside me says: 'Don't give up!' Somehow I discover that the abyss that is between me and my husband is the same one that separated me from other men in the past. Finally, when I'm desperate and honest enough, I have to concede that it's is not his fault, and it wasn't the other men's either. At this point of our marriage I feel as if I am in the middle of a township in South Africa or by the old wall between East and West – wanting desperately to bring people together even though they are as far apart as they could possibly be.

Now my husband and I meet more often at the boundaries of our wounds, talk to each other and slowly begin to view the world with curiosity rather than fear and defensiveness. I start researching relationships and read every book I can on the subject. I attend workshops and start my own psychotherapist training. More and more often my husband and I dare to express our individual truth to each other. Saying out loud how distant we feel from each other actually makes us feel closer again. With increasing courage we talk to our friends about our dismal marriage and find that other people aren't doing any better. That's such a relief! Now we begin to feel closer to each other *and* to others.

My husband is at home more often now, while I have started working again, this time as a fully trained psychotherapist. I am working with people who have reached a dead end in their jobs, just as I did as a manager. Finally, it is people who are at the centre of my work.

I begin to understand that everything we have dealt with ourselves can be passed on to others. My zigzag search for a fulfilling job now makes sense. And at the same time my marriage is beginning to come to life again. Success and fulfilment arrive in tandem.

Yet again the various aspects of my life somehow converge miraculously. The problems in my marriage lead me to a seminar with Dr Chuck Spezzano. I find myself sitting there, with 150 other people, and all I know is that he is a renowned relationship specialist from America and has written many books. I haven't read any of them.

By about ten minutes into his lecture I am feeling so moved that I can't hold back my tears. That guy up there seems to know everything about me. He must have been an invisible spy in our house for years, because every case story, every example, every joke shows that he knows my husband and me inside out. And he mentions important relationship mechanisms and rules in such a matter-of-fact way – theories that I have mulled over for a long time but never really been sure of. I am shaken and touched and at the same time liberated.

For three days I abandon myself to my tears and a stirring deep inside. Then I realize that I have received an answer to the most important questions in my professional and my private life. Whatever problem life has presented me with, it has always boiled down to how I love myself. Both my marriage and my work have pointed me in that direction, but never has it been shown to me as clearly and in such detail. I have always known the answers, but I have never trusted them. But when Chuck Spezzano focused on them, a new world of understanding finally unfolded and solidified inside me. Now I am happy and eager to explore it further.

My way of working changes once more. And my relationship with my husband changes once more. We tackle the next layer of our marriage. We explain even more clearly how alien we have become to each other. In return, we give each other understanding and support, rather than fighting. The new awareness of our differences and desires means we need fewer words, but at the same time our communication improves radically. Our friends can't believe it. 'Who would have thought...?' Our new-found strength and love can't be hidden. We now routinely come across as new lovers.

At the same time, hardly a day goes by without somebody telling me about difficulties in their relationship. More and more men and women seem to be stuck in a dead-end street.

Sometimes I feel bruised and battered by the sheer weight of it. Yesterday they'd be talking about the weather; today there's nothing but separation and bitterness. 'My wife has just left me. She's moved in with her lover.' In some cases there are four young children, in others both partners are having an affair. Sometimes there's just emptiness between them, at other times a war zone. It is a bit like an epidemic, a slow but unstoppable disease that ends more and more often in death by divorce. Relationships are ending more quickly, more frequently and more and more spectacularly. I see it happening to my friends, neighbours and colleagues. None of them wants to split up but they have all given up on their relationships and feel under pressure to take the final drastic step.

Among my clients the issue emerges only indirectly, and often furtively at first. Many men come to me for help in their quest for success and fulfilment, but after one or two assessment sessions we usually find that everything revolves around relationships – relationships with their colleagues, their workmates and bosses and, most surprisingly for my clients, their partners. At that point many of them sigh deeply, then they lose control and the tears begin to flow because the true centre of the storm has swept right through their bedroom.

Together with these long-suppressed feelings, they experience a deep insight. They have finally arrived at the top of their career ladder, yet what they are doing is a long way from their original aspirations and needs and has become an end in itself. And they can see how far they have moved from their partners and families in the process. And how they wish to reconnect their personal and their professional goals. Very often, when the draining partnership difficulties are finally allowed to take centre-stage in the talks, the single-minded career focus breaks down. Suddenly my clients want to talk to their partners again and even bring them to the sessions.

In my practice I am confronted more and more often with relationship problems that I have experienced myself. More and more couples come to me feeling just as hopeless and despairing as I once did. Hardly anybody wants to separate. Hardly anybody understands how their relationship got into such a state. But most have given up on it and are full of guilt and worry about their children.

Now I find I have turned into a relationship specialist, even though I have never consciously chosen to do so, nor advertised myself as such. It just happened the way a riverbed is gouged out by the flow of the water. My marriage was the source; books and workshops the first snowmelt floods. Chuck Spezzano was a deluge, and my clients a constant stream. They became my teachers. With each of their questions I realized that what I had experienced in my marriage had its own hidden rules. That private and professional relationships and racial conflicts are all ruled by the same laws. That relationships can only be understood, and lived, when plumbed to their depths. That the problems in a relationship have to be understood as an opportunity to heal. That separation doesn't bring healing, only delays it.

This book is meant to carry the river further. It is my way of expressing my gratitude for the gift of love in my heart. I will rejoice to the bottom of my heart if, though it, I am able to reach people whose relationship is in trouble, communicate to them some of the hope, the love and the courage that I have found and encourage them to try and rediscover those things in their own relationships.

Who is this book for?

This book is for people who are in an established but unsatisfactory relationship. For people who are in a love triangle or facing divorce. For people who are cheating on their partners or being cheated on. For people who leave their partners time after time or who are left time after time. For people who are hoping to make their relationship better but don't want to go to couple therapy or haven't found the right therapist. For people who have been on the path of suffering for a long while.

If this is you, maybe you have become cynical and just see your marriage as a matter of routine. Maybe you have given up all hope of finding intimacy with your partner. Maybe something inside you wants to recapture your old feeling of love. Maybe you are desperate because you have a secret lover and are haunted by guilt and concern for your children or your partner. Maybe you are already contemplating divorce but are frightened of saying the word out loud or of being kicked out of your home.

Whatever is wrong with your relationship, in my experience there are only two ways of dealing with it: either you feel so suffocated that you believe running away is your only way out, or you repress even the slightest unease and behave like the three monkeys who see nothing, hear nothing and say nothing. Check out what fits your situation...

Are you drained and dispirited?

Does everything seem OK on the outside but inside you feel frozen and dispirited? Are you sometimes overwhelmed by a dull feeling of 'Is this it?' Is everything just – but only just –

ticking over? Does it seem as though you and your partner are acting out a charade? Is your partner the last person to know how you really feel? Are you afraid that other people might notice how dishonest your relationship is? When you are out for dinner or with friends do you presume that other people are much happier than you? Are you trying harder and harder but getting nowhere? Has your sex life died a death – is it just a mechanical process or do you require new tricks to work up some interest? Do you feel drained? Do you have a lover? Are you dreaming of true love or at least a thrilling affair? Are you worried about your children? Are you scared of having to leave your partner? Frightened of losing your dream? Fearing the truth in your heart?

Or are you in an eternal rush?

Are you much too busy to deal with your relationship? Do you dislike any discussion about feelings? Is your inner life nobody's business? Are you sometimes scared of being abandoned? Do you think your partner doubts their feelings for you? Do you suspect that they have a lover? Have you discovered that they have? Are you throwing yourself into more work, new hobbies and countless activities so that no time is left for your partner? Do you feel excluded, beleaguered or driven out of the house? Do you feel that nothing you ever do is good enough for your partner? Are you succumbing to affairs that you don't really want? Are you numbing yourself with alcohol, food, drugs, TV, computers or other addictions – addictions which get stronger in good company or when you are alone?

If some of this or all of it is true for you, then you don't need to finish your relationship but to do a lot of work on yourself. You need to make an honest decision to heal. You don't need a Mr or Ms Right, but to be ruthlessly honest and courageous in confronting your relationship. And you need willpower, understanding, patience and a lot of practice.

PART I
THE MUNDANENESS
OF MARRIAGE

1

It doesn't matter who you marry

It doesn't matter who you marry. All you ever end up with is yourself, after all. The other person is always just the backdrop against which you check out your own unmet needs, your own ability to love, your own barriers and hurts, your own vitality, and, most of all, the deep inner rift between your desires and fears. No partner can 'make' you happy, or guarantee your self-esteem and self-confidence. So, whoever you meet, in the end you always encounter yourself. That's why, in my opinion, you might just as well stay with the partner you're with at the moment, no matter how disagreeable this may seem to you now. There is a lot of work to be done on the rut you're in, on the coldness, the anger, hatred and disgust – work to be done on *yourself!*

I am fully aware that this hypothesis will immediately raise howls of disbelief. After all, haven't we been taught from an early age that Miss Right meets Mister Right and then they live happily ever after? Most of the time, however, the fairy-tale ends on the wedding day. And the day-to-day reality of married life only kicks in *after* the wedding. And more and more marriages end long before the 'ever after'.

In the UK nearly 40 per cent of all marriages end in divorce. The most recent figures show that almost 170,000 people were divorced in 2004. The figures have been rising since the early nineties. All those people got married because they had been searching for something and they believed that they had found it in their partners. Later they got divorced because they hadn't found it after all. Their partner had turned out to be a fake – not at all what had been promised on the fancy packaging. Marriage felt like a big con.

Most divorces are unnecessary

I am confident that at least 70 per cent of all divorces need not happen. And that it doesn't matter who you marry, because all you ever meet up with is yourself! With this admittedly provocative hypothesis I'd like to nudge you into seeing marriage from a slightly different angle. Marriage is not a romance, gift-wrapped. The true meaning of marriage is the balancing of the inner conflicts of two people, and as such it is a place where deep healing can take place and authentic, generous love can be found. Some philosophers claim that life is a school. If that is true, then intimate relationships and marriages are a kind of élite university. They are where you face your most difficult tests, where you can learn and grow faster than anywhere else – and where you can gain the greatest rewards.

This is what nature intended – however many fairytales and their Hollywood successors might try to make us believe otherwise. It's at the heart of a marriage that the most challenging dynamic of life lies hidden. It's a form of paradox: even though the inherent potential of an intimate bond is more inclusive than in any other form of relationship, nowhere do our weaknesses stand out more sharply than in a committed long-term relationship. It is there that we are forced to discover that we are always missing something – our better half – and that we are *only* a man, *only* a woman.

Everybody is born either as a man or as a woman, and so from birth we are polarized. From our very first moments, we are not whole – we are either this or that, male or female. From our very first moments we long for physical, emotional and spiritual union with the opposite part. This search for our other half is part of us, a longing that is practically written into our genetic code. Every cell in our body drives us into this search, until we finally meet somebody who seems to be what we are missing. At last we are a couple, and we marry. Our longing seems to be over. At last we feel complete.

But after a few years of living together, how often does a couple appear to be complete? How connected and whole are the partners? How often do they feel harmonious and joyful? How often are they able to communicate on a deep and meaningful level? Do you know any long-term partners who actually appear to be inspired by the feeling of being complemented by each other? How many couples accept their differences as a challenge to be more compassionate and generous? How many couples regard tensions between them as opportunities for better understanding? If we believe the divorce statistics quoted above, we might come to the conclusion that it's only a matter of time before living with another human being becomes fairly unbearable. That instead of bringing us happiness, unity and the closeness that we had hoped for on our wedding day, living with someone actually takes away any hope of fulfilment and respect for the opposite sex.

This book is about happiness – about happiness and harmony in relationships. It claims that those feelings can grow over the years. It will show that we are consistently able to nurture this kind of happiness. And it wants to dismantle the belief that all you need to achieve such bliss is the right partner. It will confirm that it is in *your power alone* to renew your relationship with life and love – but to do this you have to focus on your inner self.

Your only real partner is yourself

The wholeness we are all seeking does exist. Only it's not where we think it is. It's not to be found in the outer world. We can only find it in ourselves, in our own inner core. Everybody is born with it, but hardly anybody can remember it. It is buried in us like the seed of a sunflower which contains all the information necessary for the growth of the plant. And a sunflower never asks itself whether it would rather be an apple tree. It simply grows into the best sunflower it can possibly be.

Human growth is less straightforward than that of a sunflower. The restrictions of our upbringing, the demands of our family and the influence of society can all act as genetic modifications on our inner seedling. Over time, they can have such a strong effect that we don't have even the faintest recollection of our original perfection. Our seedling has been lost to view in a fog of interference, restrictions, demands and challenges. And we lack the roots and natural impulses which we could use as guides. We have lost the feeling of connection. And what we don't understand is that it is not external connections that we lack but ones inside ourselves. We have lost the link to our own source, our natural, powerful and intuitive spirit. So we build a protective shell around our inner emptiness, and this becomes the role that we play, the assumed personality.

Sometimes we identify so much with this outer persona that over the course of time we forget who we really are. We ask ourselves whether it's better to be an apple tree than a sunflower, and whether it was wrong to be a sunflower in the first place.

Without any contact with our real selves we are continually searching for something, feeling unsure of ourselves and torn by our contradictory needs. We yearn for freedom, but desire closeness. We seek passion, then are frightened by it. Lifted by our dreams, we are dragged back down by our problems. Generosity alternates with greed. All sorts of contradictions, conscious and unconscious, cherished and rejected, shake us to and fro and push us back and forward through life. We want to get away from it all, but feel duty-bound to care for others. Every fibre in our being wants to explode and be wild, but our upbringing won't allow it. The sensuous woman in us yearns for unbridled physical love, but the motherly side has to be responsible for everyone. The powerful hero dreams of freedom and adventure, but the little boy is glad when someone looks after him, cooks for him and organizes his day.

When we are trying to find happiness in a relationship with another person, we are really looking for harmony and balance in ourselves. We are looking for a way back to our real being. We are searching for the wholeness of the seed, but we often don't even know if it exists any more. Our most precious treasure is hidden behind a fog of tension. On the one hand this is the result of so many of our feelings remaining repressed and unprocessed, locked away like animals in a cage. On the other, it is because parts of our being have not been acknowledged and are now fighting with each other in our unconscious mind. The result is chaos and a lack of direction.

But this inner mayhem does not reach our consciousness in a clearly defined way. All we feel is that there is something missing in our lives. So we look for it outside ourselves. We start looking for our better half, our soul mate, the one person who is made for us. Nearly all of us secretly hope to find bliss in a partnership with someone who complements us, supports us, understands us, attracts us and balances us – who makes us whole.

Lies, corsets and other passion-killers

In order to find and to keep this ideal person, our better half, we present ourselves at our best, of course. And that's where the problems start. In order to look our best, we show off all those aspects of ourselves which we deem presentable and acceptable. After a while, we do it automatically, especially if we have been hurt and felt unaccepted many times in the past. In the end, we play our role so well that we completely forget about the natural wholeness of our little seedling.

So, when we meet a new partner, we are only presenting those aspects of ourselves we deem to be acceptable. On an unconscious level we are also trying to do justice to all the demands of family and society. And at the same time we are trying to hide the 'less attractive' side of our personality both from others and from ourselves. This hide-and-seek only works as long as nobody gets really close to us.

A recent film showed a young woman preparing for a long-awaited date with the man of her dreams. She was standing in front of a mirror wearing a figure-hugging dress. In one hand she was holding a tiny, sexy, lacy slip. In the other she was holding a flesh-coloured stretch corset which reached from her stomach down to her thighs. She faced a grim choice.

Wearing the corset, she would look slim and fit. But what if the date turned into the night of all nights and her dream lover discovered the flesh-coloured monster while undressing her? But if she chose the sexy little slip he would see her tummy bulging straightaway and that might prevent him from taking things further anyway.

Nothing exposes our little secrets more shamelessly, nothing reveals our little subterfuges more bluntly than an intimate relationship. The closer we allow ourselves to become to another person, the less we are able to control ourselves and to function in the way we would like. In fact we experience the most unattractive side of ourselves. We get angry and moody. We feel hurt, misunderstood and powerless. We threaten or withdraw, we cling and moan, we run away. The more we open our heart, the more vulnerable we become, and the more we try to defend ourselves, the more of our own hideous nature rises to the surface. But all the other person does is take your dress off – not make you look fat. In all fairness, it is vitally important that we look at ourselves honestly and learn to accept ourselves exactly as we are.

This means having the courage to plunge into all the aspects of ourselves that we don't like, that we try to ignore, that we detest, dismiss and finally repress. But if we don't explore them and accept them with an open heart, we will continue to drive away all the people who bring them to the surface – and that means anyone who gets close to us. So we need to look under our own clothes, to take care of our own problem areas and eventually to transform them. Transforming does not mean banishing completely. It means recognizing the real essence of something and turning it into a different shape or form. In the case of a spare tyre, it means exploring whether it might make sense on a deeper level and even fulfil a purpose.

A therapist colleague told me about a client who was overweight. She had tried all sorts of methods to lose weight but without real success. During therapy she discovered that she always put on the pounds when she really wanted to commit to a partner. For a while she explored her core beliefs about men. She had to acknowledge that she had the same negative beliefs as her mother, who had been left by her father shortly after she was born. Eventually she began to suspect that her layers of fat were a very efficient defence mechanism. They prevented her from getting close to someone who, in her opinion, would only leave her anyway.

Then something really made clear the link between men and her weight. She had to go to Egypt on business for a few months – a country where curvaceous women are highly appreciated. When she came back and restarted therapy, she had lost quite a lot of weight. 'The pounds just dropped off me!' she told the therapist. 'Suddenly I wasn't hungry any more...' Once more her body had looked after her. Once more it had managed to keep men at bay. Only this time that had meant losing weight. Now the woman fully recognized that her body had only obeyed her mind by being overweight, but it still took a little while before she was ready to meet a man without her carapace of fat.

We all hate our rolls of fat, whether they are physical, spiritual or emotional. They show others how imperfect we are. They make us angry and ashamed of ourselves. And we attack them with corsets. If that doesn't work, we try to get rid of them entirely. We give up smoking, start dieting, drink less and show only our best side to our partner. But we never, ever dream of admitting that we feel hurt and inadequate. Or that we give in to the sweet temptation of chocolate or stuff ourselves with jelly babies and crisps because we feel alone and helpless. Or that we loosen up with a cigarette or a drink because we feel inhibited and uptight. We don't want to be weak and we don't want to have any rolls of fat. So we fight against our weaknesses, our faults and in the end ourselves. But anyone who has tried to battle an addiction with willpower alone knows this rarely works in the long term. We can be disciplined for a while, but in the end we always give in.

Addictions, dependencies, cravings...

The way to get rid of an addiction for good is different. For one thing, the withdrawal process clarifies that it is not the cigarette, the chocolate or the wine that gives you the good feeling. Regardless of what you use, it only serves to cover up a bad feeling, an inner tension. The resulting good feeling isn't really good, as it only masks the bad feeling. The bad feeling doesn't really disappear – you only get distracted from it for as long as the effect of the addictive substance or behaviour lasts. This is also true for most relationships, in which we consume our partners like a drug to combat our inner emptiness.

As soon as we acknowledge this link, the relentless cycle of every addiction – including our dependency on attention and relationships – becomes clear. Therefore it is much more important to explore the real core of our dependency rather than the distraction from our inner pain.

All addictions are good intentions. At the root of the word is the verb 'to add'. We want to add something to our life, whether it is a partner, food, drink, tobacco or drugs. When we binge eat, we are really looking for warm, nurturing physical contact. Alcohol helps us to release our hardened and suppressed feelings. After a few glasses we loosen up, relax and become less inhibited. Cigarettes are supposed to add freedom and adventure to life – we need one when we're on the telephone, when we're talking and thinking. And our partner is supposed to be the ultimate panacea – the one and only person who can make us feel whole.

At some point in our lives, our original feeling of completeness was disrupted. It was not satisfied, or was condemned or rejected by others, and we couldn't bear the pain that caused. So we cut ourselves off from those needs and made ourselves believe that we didn't need them any more. The pain had gone, and nobody could hurt us again. But deep inside a niggling emptiness lurked. Without real feelings and meaningful contact with others, we could never be complete again. Still, addictions filled the gaping hole and everything was fine.

Most of us can carry on like this for a while, but sooner or later we all have to recognize that we have entered a vicious circle. We are not really getting anything out of our addictions, but we need more and more of them. Even then we can only be distracted temporarily. If we are honest, we have to acknowledge that deep down, beneath all these distractions, our inner emptiness has grown, that every attempt to calm, numb and liberate ourselves is only short-lived, that no partner can be right for us in the long run, and that we need more and more of our particular drug.

We can only heal our wounds when we dare to feel the emotions we have numbed, face what we have tried to distract ourselves from and find what we really wanted to add to our lives through our addiction. And then *we* can give ourselves what we didn't receive earlier. If we dare to take this path, we can transform our addiction into a power that truly adds something to our own selves.

The same is true for the rejected or repressed parts of our personality. Over time, one after the other, like Russian dolls, we have taken on a whole range of roles. We have tried to be a loving partner, a caring parent, a helpful colleague and a loyal friend. We were taught that it was good to be all those things and integrated that entire catalogue of demands into our personal value system. But what if we can't meet all those standards and expectations?

When we were very young we learned that, depending on our behaviour, we were either good children or bad children. And since then we have also learned to hide all the bad things about ourselves. But try as we might to comply with our image of a good person, deep inside we have totally different needs. As children we wanted to be wild and noisy, to try things out, to have everything *now!* And as adults we sometimes, in a quiet moment, yearn for passion, dream of doing something really wild or want to shout at everybody, and those unappeasable needs relentlessly drive us to consumerism. Depending on how disciplined we are, we resist those desires. We bite our tongue and present our best aspects to the world. If that doesn't work, we start building a diversion route for all our 'bad' desires, longings, feelings and needs. We stuff ourselves with food, get drunk or allow ourselves at least once, in secret, to be a passionate and un-bridled lover.

The more we pretend that this unacceptable part of ourselves doesn't exist, and the harder we try to hide it, to reject it and to compensate for it by playing out a 'good' role or by simply repressing and forgetting it, it just won't go away. Quite the opposite – everything that we have banished from our conscious awareness emerges in other places, often in a distorted form. It turns up in close relationships in particularly full force. All those supposedly distasteful parts of ourselves are reflected back to us most accurately in our most intimate encounters. So, in our relationships, we lose control, we hide, we cheat, we let ourselves go or we greedily demand more. And we are outraged. This can't be our fault! Our partner has driven us to distraction, has 'made' us unhappy and practically driven us away. We ourselves are doing everything we can to have a loving relationship. We are completely unaware of all those 'bad', destructive or sabotaging feelings and thoughts deep inside us, and we don't want to hear about them either.

I can't repeat it often enough: there is only one way of real healing, only one way to an authentic and successful love relationship – we have to confront the abyss within us with courage and honesty.

This doesn't take years of psychotherapy or agonizing self-analysis. All it needs is a real closeness to your partner and a true willingness to explore your inner self. When this leads you to discover unwanted qualities and hidden fears in yourself and your behaviour, you will begin to see the difficulties in your relationship in a different light. Then you will get an idea of how the deeply hidden, negative and maybe even destructive core beliefs within you mirror truthfully what happens on the surface. Although you long for attention and love, for example, on an unconscious level you don't feel worthy of it. Although you yearn for closeness, you prevent it at the same time. You might even begin to find that you have never felt worthy of being treated any other way than badly. You might realize that your relationships have followed the same pattern time and again and understand that you cannot stop compulsively recreating this pattern simply by choosing a new partner.

More of the same – the celebrity phenomenon

I love reading the tabloids. The lives of so-called celebrities are full of things the rest of the world won't allow. We may all secretly dream of doing such things, but probably don't have the means to do so, and we just love to point the finger at those who do.

From Hollywood to the Centre Court, from Monaco to LA, we can observe something I like to call 'the celebrity phenomenon': a deep and meaningful relationship followed by a surprising separation (surprising to the outside world at least) and a quick succession of bafflingly similar affairs. Like an old LP with a scratch, whether at a film premiere, an Academy Award ceremony or the Oktoberfest, it's the same story over and over again. The record gets stuck at exactly at the same place, whether it be film stars, royalty or sports personalities. After a love affair which frequently ends in marriage and then in divorce, there is a whole series of partners who look like clones of the first one. Celebrities all seem to be on the search for something they really didn't want in the first place – a new edition of the first relationship. With some celebrities, after the first divorce, photographers have recorded about half a dozen replacements – all interchangeable. Obviously the stars reached their intimacy limits in their first relationship and couldn't cross them with any of the new partners either.

Every now and again the tabloids put the photos of all the exes together, and then it's not only the gossip columnists who are asking themselves why someone like, say, Boris Becker didn't simply stay with his wife Barbara and their children. Why did he continually search for the same type of exotic woman when he couldn't actually live with any of them? But if you read the autobiography he wrote after this very turbulent phase in his life you will realize that Boris was looking for something that Barbara and all her successors couldn't give him: he was looking for himself.

Many celebrities have lost their true selves while playing a role for the outside world. And when we can't see ourselves any more, we seek more connection and recognition outside ourselves. But if we can't recognize our own feelings, we can't empathize with the people close to us either. We look for the feelings, but we can't find them. All we can do is follow a series of inner patterns which are partly contradictory – until we meet our true self.

The first thing we do on our search for happiness, though, is not look for our true self but for another person. And when that relationship fails, we look for yet another person. The celebrities we read about in the tabloids may have more opportunities, more temptations and more independence than we do. But deep inside, they too are haunted by the same phenomenon as everybody else: a conscious desire for a relationship sabotaged by an unconscious programme.

Our most important task is to detect and acknowledge this conflict. If we shy away from this inner work, if we don't explore why at a certain point in a relationship the record gets stuck, then it will simply start all over again until we finally withdraw with a broken heart or turn into a notoriously heartless Casanova.

This work can't be done by our conscious mind alone. Even if we decide never to have a relationship like our last one, vow never to go through anything like that ever again, swear never to want anyone like that ever again and then consciously choose a very different type of person from our previous partner, believing that this time everything will be different, our hidden patterns, beliefs and wounds will ensure that everything repeats itself all over again.

Why everything stays the same when everything is supposed to change

When Kim first came to me she had just split up with her long-term partner because he had had a string of affairs with ever-shorter gaps in between. Finally, a new man saved her from the arms of this cold-hearted Don Juan. Everybody was happy, because the new partner was obviously so much more loving and caring. He really fought to win her, and eventually they got married and had children. Years went by and then this man seemed to undergo a complete metamorphosis. In the end he even drove the same type of car as Kim's ex. And at one point he cheated on her in an even more scandalous and inconsiderate way than her old lover had done.

Kate's first husband had beaten her and sponged off her. Her friends said, 'He was selfish and out of control.' Everybody agreed that she deserved better. Her next boyfriend seemed so different! He was softer, more empathic and generous. Things looked good. But eventually Kate's bruises couldn't be overlooked any more. This man too had beaten her. When they separated she had to leave her home and was again left with more or less nothing. With the third man a miracle seemed to happen. This guy was a successful manager and was besotted with her. He signed over half his property to her. But during the course of the marriage he somehow lost his fortune and had a nervous breakdown. He beat her up and, as the co-owner and guarantor, she lost everything they owned together.

You might think those stories are exceptional or incredible coincidences, yet relationships follow very precise laws that your conscious mind doesn't recognize or comprehend. Each and every one of your inner beliefs, your fears and defences, no matter how deeply buried they are in your soul, will manifest in your relationship. You can dream of your ideal woman until the cows come home, but if you are unconsciously afraid of women or even harbour doubts about female integrity from generations back, these inner beliefs will turn up right in front of you. You might think this is an exaggeration, but during the course of this book you will come to understand that time and again you recreate all the unsatisfactory relationships that you don't really want.

Princes turning into frogs – brilliant!

The fact that there are precise laws ruling relationships might sound alarming. Romantic illusions might have to be ditched. They will. But when romantic illusions go, true love can come in.

To begin with, though, we wait for a noble prince to appear on a white charger or hope that a beautiful princess will let her hair down for us. We search moats and courtyards for perfect partners and at best discover only average men and women. And if, in spite of our disappointment, we get involved with them, they turn into frogs.

A wise man once said, 'The moment you fall in love with someone is the moment they start turning into a frog.' But that's no reason to be anxious, according to the same wise man: 'There's nothing bad about frogs – frogs are wonderful. The world is full of frogs.' He thinks we should be happy that our dream prince or princess has turned out to be a frog. 'Because real princes and princesses would never fall for frogs like us. Just accept that you are only a frog yourself and be really curious about the other frog.' That's his solution to all romantic dilemmas.

In terms of relationships, my favourite fairytale is *The Beauty and the Beast*. It suggests that you shouldn't leave your dried-up old frog or send your nagging and shrivelled old frog wife packing. Instead, if you love the ugly and scary beast at your side with all your heart and passion, in the end, through your unconditional love, it will turn into a prince or princess.

We all know how we want people to be: beautiful, strong, clever, sensitive, loving, educated – we have a whole list of demands, based on our upbringing. A prince for one person might be a beast for another. In any case, we judge our partners according to our own personal expectations. And whenever they don't match up, we call them frogs or beasts.

Real love, however, is nothing to do with an ideal. Parents of disabled children know this. They love them not because of what they are, they simply love them, and often more uncon-ditionally than they could ever have imagined. But it's the same with healthy children too – you know how deeply and devotedly you can love those whingeing, crying monsters and that in your heart they are always little princes and princesses.

Couples, parents, lovers

Have you ever asked yourself whether you would leave your children? But if your partner didn't make the grade, you'd leave, wouldn't you? 'Absolutely!' some of you will say. You know people who have found a more harmonious and peace-ful relationship second time around. I know them too. Some of them went through a phase of deep transformation and personal growth before the new relationship began. Most of them, though, simply distanced themselves from the trigger for their pain, not from the pain itself. Many of those people have children with their first partners. Today, although they are no longer a couple, they are still parents with their ex-partner and not yet married to the new one.

What I want to say is, being married means being father, mother *and* lover – it means playing every role and sharing every part of yourself. In church weddings it is sometimes said: 'When the two of you become one.' This doesn't mean romantically melting into each other, or two ideal partners meeting each other, or being joined at the hip from now on and not having any personal space. Becoming one in this sense means loving the otherness in your partner in order to experience your own love more profoundly. It means being fully responsible for yourself – including your own space and boundaries – in order to meet another person as truthfully as possible. It is all about recognizing what the other person is really like – and that may be just as average as you are. It means acting differently, thinking differently, accepting weaknesses and failures in the other person and integrating them.

Being a couple is one of the most important ways of maturing and accepting another person. First and foremost, it entails personal growth. In its deepest spiritual sense, being a couple means overcoming the illusion of separateness – not physical or geographical separateness, but the personal separation of rejecting, judging and condemning.

Divorce means separating from your old wounds

Being a couple also means having responsibilities, caring, giving and nurturing. Being lovers means receiving, discovering, playing and experiencing abandonment. Life is never entirely one or the other. Within us, the two principles alternate too.

When we divide our life in two – when we are a parent in one relationship and a lover in another – then we transfer our inner conflict to the outside. Our relationship to our former marriage partner is ultimately about money, duties, education, agreements and responsibility. With the new partner, passion, freedom and a sense of adventure enter our life. With that person, we often leave behind the expectations of family and society and finally allow a long-repressed part of ourselves to come to the fore.

With the old partner we often did things according to our upbringing, but found ourselves in a cul-de-sac of repetitiveness and routine. Unconsciously, we ended up in all sorts of old familiar patterns. Sometimes we even brought up our children the same way our parents brought up us, in spite of deciding to do everything differently! The old partner somehow embodies this former 'home' – the place where we weren't allowed to be ourselves. By divorcing, we now leave this old home and feel liberated. But the tragic thing is that as long as we are not aware of the old patterns and hurts of our former home and have not healed them, we will continue along the same path. In the meantime, however, we feel free at last with the new partner while all our pain remains associated with the ex-partner. We have distributed our inner tensions among two people, and one seems right and the other wrong.

Often the new relationship keeps its magic as long as it stays free from commitments. Take a look at how new relationships change when issues such as children and money emerge. And take a closer look at the influence of old relationships. Both parties can hurt each other for a long, long time afterwards. Destructive, sad, revengeful, guilty or nostalgic thoughts, problems and tensions can give rise to an endless amount of passion and commitment between former partners for years – sometimes for the rest of their lives. I know many separated couples who over the course of time have discovered that no chucking out, no moving away, no divorce can effect a separation in the heart, and that rejection and hatred can be just as binding as love.

You might say, 'But the solution can't possibly be to stay together at all costs. You can't stay with a man who has beaten you up or with a wife who has cheated on you.' No, that isn't the solution. I don't advocate sticking it out until death do you part, or going through the motions for the sake of it when both parties left emotionally ages ago. I get sad when I meet couples who are still living together but are further apart than others who have had the courage to face the consequences and separate. Often people end up chained to each other rather than following a common path together.

There is an old saying: 'If you want to get rid of your chains, love them.' To be honest, it took me years to understand what this meant and to apply it to my marriage. Maybe my experience will help you to achieve this more quickly. I am not pleading either for divorce or for staying together at all costs. I passionately believe in vitality, authenticity and truth, and the aim of this book is to inspire you to recapture your own self. I hope it also encourages you to uncover the lies you have been living and to find your own truth behind them. On this journey you will discover the love and life in your own heart and in those of the people around you. This journey to yourself is also the way to revive the power, love and passion in your relationship.

The new relationship – 'I yearned for life!'

After 30 years of marriage, a well-known German politician embarked on a new relationship, admitting, 'For a long time I confused politics with life.' Like many men, for decades he had drawn a sharp dividing line between his emotional life and his work, between his real self and his public persona. Now he seemed to undergo a transformation. He shaved off his beard and turned up radiant with his new wife, wearing stylish glasses and fashionably loose suits. 'I yearned for life,' he stated, shrugging off all criticism and jokes.

Many divorces are the result of people being unable to play out their restrictive roles any more. Men in particular find that the armour that they have put on in the course of their career suddenly gets too tight. It seems as if they divorce their wives in order to leave their own history behind. The German politician also looked as if he had had to leave his marriage and family in order to be real for once – to be himself. The new woman was his second attempt to find himself by means of a relationship. For her it was the third time.

If such a search for the self has not developed organically but been triggered by an outside event, if it arises because of another person, then the impact is felt in a radical and explosive way in all areas of life. A transformation that might have taken years of conscious decisions, small steps towards personal development and courageous insights now swirls like a hurricane through a well-organized life.

It is not the new partner that makes the relationship between the two people different from their former experiences, however, but their increased willingness to communicate and their courage to bear the consequences of their love. The attraction of the new partner triggers a passionate process of opening up which singles never have enough strength and courage to do on their own.

A new partner challenges us and reminds us of the ideal that we have lost sight of. We discover something of ourselves in the other person, something that we have wanted for a long time, something we buried early on the long road to adaptation. When at last we experience this part of ourselves in the outside world, something stirs inside us too. But it's only if we have strayed a long way from our real path that we are finally ready to step out of the small and restricted space of our old relationship – and step beyond our own limitations.

When asked in an interview what valuable insights he had gained in 30 years in politics, the German politician replied, 'Never jeopardize your convictions, your character and your private happiness by what you do.'

Discover your own strength, spark your own passion

New love can ignite the hurricane of change, but it can also have other triggers. Often people experience it after a serious crisis or a near-fatal illness. Such dramatic events either drive the victims into complete paralysis or back to their real path, their old self and their strength. Time and again you read of people who in terrible circumstances find their courage, their passion and their fighting spirit.

People who have overcome a strong addiction can also develop a strength that nobody would have suspected. As addicts they search for physical, emotional or mental satisfaction, but only find an even stronger addiction. During the withdrawal process they have the opportunity of analyzing every aspect of their situation and uncovering every layer of paralysis, weakness, greed and lovelessness. Once they succeed, they can finally discover their true strength, sometimes even their true inner divinity, and bring it back into their life. The place inside them that was formerly eaten up by the addiction can now overflow with strength, passion and creativity.

Any of us can experience this. We can do it with our current partner, but if we do, we ourselves will have to raise the storm that will whip up the waves that will carry us on. We will need great courage to speak our own truth and to live it at the risk of hurting our partner and everybody else around us. We will have to leave our comfort zone. We will have to be prepared to be neither loved nor understood. And we will have to be prepared to stay with our partner because every minute we will also have to be prepared to leave.

Nietzsche called marriage a 'dialogue'. In order to keep this dialogue going, in his view, the partners would have to enter into a continuous 'radical conversation'. They would have to be prepared to share their innermost thoughts and feelings – to confront their fears and respect their differences.

I don't maintain that this is an easy way. I'm not claiming that it is easier to stay together than to separate. But I think it is more fulfilling. And I'm paying this homage to good old marriage for pragmatic rather than moral reasons. My life has convinced me that there is no bigger task than overcoming our own nature, time and again, in order to know it more fully. And to truly encounter our own nature we need to truly encounter another person. And that will ultimately show us that we need nothing from them.

What I mean by this is that whenever we believe that we need something, we are indirectly stating that we are weak and incomplete. Every time we discover that we don't need something any more, our self-esteem and our ability to love grow and, paradoxically enough, bring fulfilment. That means that everything we can let go of during the course of our life – beginning with the mother's breast – makes us richer and freer and more secure. Growth means letting go of our neediness little by little and not constantly needing something new.

In terms of relationships, we always seem to be looking for something that we are missing: the ideal partner, a lot of attention and love. But though we are apparently looking for our better half, we are really looking to heal ourselves.

If we stay in a relationship, and truly understand what that is about, we will give ourselves the best chance to grow and to heal. After all, the best therapist in the world can't tap into our repressed feelings as quickly and precisely as our partner. They manage to activate our shadow side every day! And even though we may hate them for it, we should be aware that they are helping us to find the demons in ourselves and to shake them off.

In such situations, if we can find the courage for a radical change of perspective, we can admit that our partner is not the cause but the trigger of our problems. Then, if we can manage to stay true to ourselves while perceiving and healing all those unwanted and unpleasant aspects of ourselves, we are doing our job. And when we deal with ourselves in such an unsparing and intensive way, we experience more and more break-throughs with our partner, a deepening love and more freedom and strength. And when we are healing our relationship in such a way, our children are automatically healing too. And when our children are healing, society as a whole is healing.

Peter Russell says that relationships are the yoga of Western society. He uses the word 'yoga' in its original sense, meaning work, particularly spiritual work. Russell's point is that we must use our relationships as a kind of meditative yoga in order to develop ourselves and our society.

Over the years I have met many people whose marriage was on the rocks. Many have since separated. I am convinced that most of them would have stood a good chance of staying together if both partners had thought more about the meaning and function of intimate relationships, their phases and laws, and if they had practised the yoga of marriage continuously, relentlessly and with trust. This *can* turn marriage into an adventure. It *can* magically transform your perception. If you do it regularly you will discover that truth, growth, openness, courage and giving are much more exciting than taking.

2

We always marry for the wrong reasons

It could be said that the reason we feel so incomplete is that we were all born either male or female. We are always either one or the other, never complete, always only half of a whole. Viewed in this light, our search for the right relationship is necessary rather than romantic. We can see that we are always lacking something, always on the lookout for something to fill our gaps.

So we remain lonely until finally Mr Right turns up or until we find love and tenderness with a new wife. Whatever form it takes, a relationship brings something into our life. Without one, we are missing out. So we are all on an eternal quest for a relationship to make us feel happy and alive.

If we make these assumptions, however, we are already in trouble. Because we need a relationship like a crutch in order not to be lonely or unhappy. And however wonderful it might appear at the outset, sooner or later those expectations will wreck it.

Two one-legged people learn to walk

A relationship like this is like a one-legged person looking for another one-legged person in order to walk. The two get together, have two legs – and walk! Problem solved. In their initial phase of bliss they may even forget that they were ever one-legged. Until one day one of them wants to change direction or speed ... and suddenly the other one is cruelly reminded of their disability. They can't walk on alone and begin to limp. They fall down. And because they had completely forgotten that they were born one-legged, they blame the other person for the limping and falling, and even for the disability itself. Most people experience this kind of scenario at some point. Suddenly there is something missing in their relationship – tenderness, support, safety, passion, attention – and it's all the other person's fault.

If you enter a relationship as only half a person and therefore think that you need someone to supply the missing bits, then paradoxically you lay the foundation for conflict and separation. Your partner cannot *make* you happy. They can count themselves lucky if they can do that for themselves. In the beginning you might be caught up in the illusion that this wonderful new person at your side is bringing wonderful new things into your life. But it is only a matter of time before you are cursing them for the very qualities you sought in the first place. Because they are withholding them from you and cannot or will not meet your expectations.

Once, in a relationship workshop, a husband and wife were standing in front of each other. There wasn't more than a foot between them. Step by step, the husband, whose marriage was in great difficulties, had walked towards his wife. In this therapeutic process, with every one of those steps – some tearful, others heavy and reluctant – he had symbolically stepped through an issue which had separated him from his wife in the past. Now he was standing in front of her, vulnerable and open, watched by a fairly large audience. Finally he was forced to look her in the eyes and to be really close to her, to see her as she really was. Then, frightened and kind of panicky, he looked at the therapist. 'I married her for the wrong reasons!' he stammered, deeply shaken.

The therapist smiled sagely. 'We all marry for the wrong reasons.'

The reasons disappear, the partner remains

Women marry men because they are successful, smart and strong, because they can kill bears, read balance sheets and are skilful in bed. Women marry men because they are exactly like their father, or completely different. Women marry men because they are the father of their child or because their friends fancy them. Women marry men because their parents have arranged it or because they will get money or a new passport for doing it.

Men marry women because all their friends find them irresistible, because they look gorgeous, have a brilliant bum or blonde hair. Men marry women because they are allowed to conquer them. Men marry women because they can manage men so well. Men marry women because they are good cooks, just like their mother – or better. Men marry women because they want a family or because they need someone who admires them. Men marry women because they want sex or are scared of being alone.

We always marry for a reason. Most of the time, though, those reasons turn out to be a curse. Successful men are never at home. Beautiful women get wrinkles and cellulite. All the reasons why we got married turn out to be delusions, change or simply disappear. Our hopes turn into greed – nothing is ever good enough. Beauty fades, success does not bring contentment. We need more success, more beauty, more attention, more care. More sex. But it's not enough. At some point we feel drained inside or that we are dying a slow death. Often our frustrating search for what we need simply ends with a new partner who promises us more satisfaction and fulfilment.

Whatever our reasons for marrying, with regard to the durability of the marriage, they are all volatile and changeable. They are really only indicators of our own inadequacy. For that reason, one of the most important steps you can take towards renewing the life of your partnership is to acknowledge the reason why you married your partner in the first place. 'Well, because I was in love!' most of you will say now. But no other sentence in the world has as many different meanings as 'I love you.' Or contains so little of the truthfulness and wholeness of the person to whom it is spoken. Or expresses so much of the subjective needs of its speaker.

'I love you' contains the word 'I'

Be brave and face up to what it means when you say 'I love you'. Whatever it is, the sentence starts with the word 'I'. This 'I' filters all our experience of love so far, all our conditioning from childhood, all our unspoken expectations and unfulfilled desires. They are all hidden in this very personal 'I love you'. Have you already guessed that this might have very little to do with your partner as a real person?

'I love you' can mean all sorts of things: 'I love you because I find you attractive.' 'I love you because you are successful and wealthy.' 'I love you because you fought for me.' 'I love you because you are so creative.' 'I love you because you have everything that I don't have.' 'I love you because you are so much like me.'

On an unconscious level your 'I love you' has countless other meanings as well. 'I love you because you are so different from the person who hurt me.' 'I love you because with you I feel as distant as I did with my father.' 'I love you because you appear as helpless as my mother.' 'I love you because I feel so worthless and you seem so rich.' 'I love you because I'm scared to be alone.'

If you really arrive at the reasons why you married your partner you will – if you are thoroughly open and honest – always come to a place where you seem to be lacking something. It is your desires and inadequacies that the other person is supposed to satisfy. So their strengths are things that *you* apparently lack. That is why your relationship problems are based on *your* deficits. They are really based on distorted and mostly repressed programs you had hardwired very early on, long before you met your partner.

The iceberg model

Everybody lives with countless emotional disturbances, both large and small. Most of them are not conscious, but they nevertheless condition our behaviour. This is not easy to understand, so here's a way of clarifying it. Put both your thumbs and forefingers together to form a little triangle. I call this the tip of the iceberg. It symbolizes the part of you that is visible to yourself and others – the part that you are conscious of. This is the part that falls in love. This is the part that believes you have met your dream man or woman, the part that one day says 'I love you' to another person. This is the part responsible for saying 'I do' at the wedding.

Now hold this finger triangle in front of your forehead and imagine that your lower arms are an extension of your fingers. Now you have the whole iceberg. The small triangle at the top between your fingers, the part that falls in love or finds its better half, only symbolizes the part that is visible above the waterline – the part that you call 'me'.

In reality this is the smallest part of you. Your real self, your more complex personality, is the larger part from the wrist to the elbows. Down here are all the things that disappeared from your consciousness or never even reached it in the first place. That's everything that was not allowed in your family. Everything you were taught was undesirable. Everything that once hurt so much that you'd rather repress or forget it than face it again. Everything that you never understood, accepted or healed. Everything that you never felt capable of. All your old patterns, early childhood experiences, pain, hurts and fears, as well as your unfulfilled potential, your unexpressed vitality and your undivided love. All the good things that were once a natural part of you but didn't find space or acceptance. Down here these things have gone bad. Formerly unexpressed power and lust, forbidden wishes and drives have turned into aggression, shame, greed and hatred, which in the end we condemn ourselves for because we never remember the good intentions behind them.

Our repressed powers are like caged tigers. The tiger itself is an elegant, lithe and powerful animal that needs to roam freely. Out in the world it is guided by its instincts and in perfect harmony with its environment. If you take away its freedom and put it in a cage, however, it turns into an unpredictable, aggressive and dangerous creature. It's the same with everything that is caged at the bottom of the iceberg – everything that we now consider dangerous, that we don't want to know about consciously or don't allow ourselves to do or feel, everything that doesn't fit our value system, our upbringing and our society, everything that once made us a 'bad' child and that today we condemn.

Of course, the iceberg model is also true for your partner. While above water – 'above the consciousness threshold' – two little icebergs are drifting across the ocean, full of mutual respect and intense longing, whispering 'I love you,' below the waterline something else is going on. It may well be that 'I love you' is turning into 'I love you if you do what I want' or 'I love you if you behave like my dad.' The little triangles are just planning their first child, while underwater the corners of the larger triangles are colliding, reopening old wounds, and two rejected villains are beginning to fight.

In reality, those presumed 'baddies' are orphaned, helpless and attention-seeking creatures following their own logic. With few exceptions most originate in our childhood, and they function and act like children. While above water we want to love our partner deeply and maturely, the hurt child underneath curls up in a corner, frightened of being abandoned. While above water we want to love and give, underneath parts of ourselves are sabotaging our plans and actively choosing negativity, separation, selfishness, fear and mistrust.

The child in us lives on

How can it be that we act in such a divided and deranged way? From birth onwards we are searching for completeness and perfection, because we are 'only' a man, 'only' a woman. But for a small child the deep elemental desire for connection is completely different from that of an adult. As children we are never searching for the right relationship, the right parents, the right acceptance. We are totally passive and receptive. We do nothing but take on board whatever is happening around us. We soak up nurturing, warmth and attention just as we do disharmony, abuse and rejection. We simply take in everything that happens and think that's what the world is like.

It is in this absolutely receptive, non-judgemental state that growth takes place. Whenever we received enough nurturing, attention and love, we grew. Whenever it was lacking, there was no growth. So, with time, a totally individual profile of replete and deficient personality parts developed, their respective world views dependent on the development phase in which they were interrupted, hurt, abused or simply not attended to. If as young babies we had to do without something fundamental, then today there is a part of us that responds and functions as a hungry, frightened, fearful or lonely baby. If we were hurt, abused or traumatized in puberty, there is a part of us that views the world as a hurt teenager. The longer-lasting and more traumatic the negative events, the more intensive the impact of those parts on our life today.

If you find it difficult to understand how this works, imagine yourself as an extended family. Remember that every time your natural growth is interrupted by hurt, lack of nourishment or trauma, part of you gets stuck and is split off. So later on, when you enter into a relationship, you always have a large family of infants, toddlers, children and adolescents along with you.

For the adult, real fulfilment is blocked when a child that got stuck during puberty is still looking for its own particular kind of fulfilment. It yearns for nurturing parents, not for a powerful, free and grown-up relationship with another person. It looks for passive closeness and a melting into another person, but lacks a clear self that can have a unique encounter with another self.

As adults, we want to act consciously and make our own decisions, but the child in us tends to react automatically. Viewing the world from the former, frozen situation, it transfers all the old feelings and blocks to the new situation and the other person. This means the inner child simply repeats the childhood patterns time and again without question, without consciousness, without intellectual distancing. This, for example, is the reason why people who have been beaten as children look for partners who will beat them – without being conscious of it at all. Similarly, children of alcoholics often marry alcoholics.

The iceberg of old stories is not only at work when these difficulties emerge in a marriage. Our inner children turn up unexpectedly in all sorts of situations. Sometimes our partner perceives them more clearly than we do. I have noticed that when some women get close to men, they can't take male authority seriously any more. A man might have an important position, expert knowledge or specialist competence, but, for instance, as one woman said, 'He might be the Emperor of China, but when he sits next to me, he is like a little boy.' Women sense intuitively that away from the official persona, parts of a man's personality can be very childlike. They might not be noticeable at first glance because they are hidden behind powerful gestures and impressive lectures, but with closeness they become more and more visible.

Even when we fall in love, our extended family of childlike personality parts has a finger in the pie. And the mechanism works with the same precision. No matter how intense our desire for a harmonious relationship with an ideal partner, we always bring our old emotional baggage with us, and without conscious awareness find ideal partners indeed: people whose pain matches ours. People with iceberg stumps like ours. People whose hidden inadequacies collide so precisely and painfully with ours that at the tip of the iceberg we are suddenly ripped from our romantic dream and react with fear, doubts, insecurity and distance.

The confusion resulting from this split between top and bottom is the ultimate reason behind a separation. I've never had a single person come to me and say clearly and categorically: 'I want to split up with my partner because I'm not interested in them any more and because they mean nothing to me.' It's always a resigned 'I have tried everything and we can't go on like this.' I constantly see people feeling ambivalent, split, involuntarily cut off or distanced. Or they rant and rave about their partner's bad behaviour and feel helpless at the same time because nothing they do is 'good enough' to get through to them. Without exception they are all searching for love, regardless of how complicated or dramatic their relationship is at that point. When couples come to see me together, the anger and bitterness, pain and suffering are linked especially closely to tears, despair and the yearning for intimacy and healing. If the couple are consciously aware of this link they often feel confused about their ambiguous feelings and ambivalent behaviour.

The woman wants passion, the child wants protection

When Catherine came to me, she felt completely devoid of femininity, passion and sensuality, and could not bear her husband to be near her any more. She didn't want him to touch her, she said, couldn't sleep with him any more and thought he was an utter failure. But Catherine was also anxious whenever her husband was late home at night. She was afraid to go on holiday or even away for a weekend on her own. She asked her husband all the time to be near her and stay with her – but when he was around she could hardly tolerate him. He got on her nerves, so she started arguments with him and nagged him mercilessly.

When Catherine told me all this she was confused and appalled at her own behaviour. After all, she had come to me because she wanted to save her marriage. She claimed to love her husband. But she also found him unbearable. And she was ashamed of her angry and vindictive attitude towards him. This inner turmoil made her feel helpless. She wondered whether she was going mad.

Catherine's story is only one of many in my practice that show a deep inner rift. Her adult relationship with her husband is troubled. That is because countless childlike desires and childlike responses are involved.

Whenever our development from infant to child, child to adolescent and adolescent to adult in our family of origin doesn't run smoothly, both mental and emotional gaps remain in our personality, like scars. Parts of us that were hurt, unfulfilled or not sufficiently protected and nurtured by our mother and father get stuck in their emotional development. Later, when we meet our partner, those childlike parts unconsciously look for healing. While the adult in us responds to our partner as an adult, the hurt and immature child in us may be needy, anxious and rejecting. Then we get confused and have doubts about our relationship.

Consciously, Catherine longs for a sexual relationship, while at the same time the anxious child in her wants to cling to Daddy. She remembers her childhood as deeply divided. There was a time 'before' and a time 'after'. With 'before' she means her years as a small child. Then her dad had played around with her and they had had fun. When Catherine talked about this physical playfulness with her father, she smiled brightly. Then, when she was about ten or eleven, this close contact had suddenly stopped. Her father had withdrawn without a word. 'I have no memory whatsoever of sitting on his lap after that time or having a cuddle,' she said.

Catherine is not the only one with such an experience. When their daughters started growing up, many fathers of our parents' generation began to feel very insecure in their physical expression towards them. Suddenly they felt inhibited and ashamed. 'How close can I get to her? What if I feel something?' It happened unconsciously, but was sharply felt by those concerned. As a result, many fathers and daughters found themselves facing a separation much too early, and it was painful for them. For many girls the development towards womanhood was sharply interrupted at this point. Unconsciously, their minds were programmed with messages such as: 'I am not attractive.' 'Men don't want me.' 'I have to be ashamed to feel physical lust.' 'I get men into difficulties with my blossoming body.' While externally the girls continued to mature, an important part of their personality got stuck.

In order to understand these dynamics properly we could say that in the case of Catherine there is not just one woman meeting her man, but many different personae. Imagine Catherine and her husband at the tip of the triangle and beneath the surface many little Catherines whispering, doubting or interrupting. At the tip of the iceberg the wife says, 'I love my husband.' Down at the bottom, meanwhile, chaos breaks out. A lively young woman yearns for passion but is disgusted by her father/husband. An adolescent girl wants attention but is not allowed to be touched any more by her father/husband. A growing child wants a cuddle, but senses physical or even sexual attraction and perceives an unspoken rule against such needs in the father/husband. There is also a toddler there, filled with the need for protection and afraid that this father/husband won't come home at night and will leave her alone at the weekend or on holiday. And a good daughter, who is ashamed because she is not as loving towards her husband as women are supposed to be. And a mother who thinks that the man is a failure because he can't meet all those childlike needs. And the grown-up Catherine thinks she must be mad.

If it's confusing just reading about all this, imagine what it's like to live with it in a day-to-day relationship! Every time two people approach each other, they set off whole armies of people inside themselves, without having the slightest clue that they are doing it. So it is totally understandable when people begin to withdraw after a few skirmishes – just to stay with the military metaphor. And if we don't split up straight-away, we often only communicate superficially, remain non-committal and refuse to get involved. That prevents a whole bunch of veterans from being mobilized and possibly fighting a losing battle.

Our partner hears what we don't say

But even when we try to ignore parts of ourselves – our heart or body, for instance – and limit our communication to empty niceties, a similar process will take place. When two people want to get involved with each other they only respond to each other's words on a superficial level. What they really respond to is the invisible current between them.

These dynamics, too, are due to our upbringing. Every family has a specific emotional atmosphere. This climate – all those emotional currents between father and mother and within the family – conditions us much more intensely than the verbalized rules we receive from our parents. Virtues may be praised and goals for life and learning defined, but the day-to-day reality may be totally different, full of ambivalence, uncertainty, even hypocrisy, distrust and arguments. As children we perceive all these disturbances, and frequently feel confused by the gap between what is happening and what our parents are actually saying.

Later on it becomes completely normal for most of us not to tell other people how we are really feeling, and we often reduce communication to a harmless minimum, an exchange of niceties. Mostly this doesn't work. Relationships between people are first and foremost a dynamic process. We hear messages, but we respond mainly to the underlying sub-text and to *how* something is expressed. For example, when we tell our partner 'I have done this or that today,' the underlying message is 'Please be proud of me ... praise me ... you can't do it anyway ... it was your task really...' Often there are a dozen or so automatically activated sub-messages underneath the main one. Sometimes we are conscious of the sub-messages we are giving out, but we don't notice the majority of them.

The tragic thing in all relationship communication is that it is the very messages that we don't perceive that cause a reaction in the other person. Your partner hears that you did this or that today, but suddenly they feel irritated and become distant. Most of the time they are not conscious of why this is happening, as you have only mentioned trivialities. Mostly they don't even realize that they have become distant. All they know is that they really wanted to see you or hear you, but somehow it hasn't worked out.

For years there was a little routine between my husband and me which was symbolic of our relationship then. Whenever he came home, he embraced me. And before he came home I looked forward to it. When he actually did it, though, I felt uncomfortable. In the beginning all I felt was a little 'Ugh...' after an embrace. Later, however, I became really tense and eventually quite angry. One day I simply pushed him away and shouted, 'Can't you even give me a real hug?' My husband was completely baffled. 'But I *am* giving you a hug!' Yes, he was. But at the same time something more was happening between us.

After that we had a huge argument and accused each other of all sorts of things. We discharged so much emotion that later, with more distance and calmness, we were able to gain new insights and a greater intimacy. We realized that I had wanted power and protection, to be held in the arms of a strong man. But with every embrace my husband had deflated like a pierced balloon. He is much taller than I am and when he embraced me he always automatically lowered his head and made himself appear smaller, so small in fact that in the end he was resting in my arms. In this embrace neither of us had anything to give. But both of us were looking to receive a caress. So every attempt had made the frustration worse and widened the inner gap. The connection between us had lessened, but our needs increased. And at this point in our marriage tenderness was not a gift, only a need.

Today we make jokes about my husband putting his head down between his shoulders while embracing me. After many hurtful encounters we can laugh about how he always wanted to be small and to cuddle up to me as if curling up in his mother's lap, while I really wanted to fall into his arms as though I was resting on my father's broad chest. Don't get me wrong – I'm not against really letting yourself go with another person and not against cuddles either. Tenderness is the lifeblood of every relationship – but it has to be something that flows from real closeness and emotional fulfilment between two grown-up people.

Time and again women tell me that after a number of years their marriage is like a physical and emotional desert. I know that feeling too. After the stormy passionate kisses of our first encounters, the hollow embraces later felt like empty packaging. The same applied to the passionless, routine 'I love you' after a while. When one day I became aware of how meaningless it sounded, it conjured up the good old times. I nostalgically thought of one rare scene during the first months of our relationship: we sat in the car, confessed our love to each other and cried because we had to separate for a whole week.

In the course of our marriage it has not been easy for us to recognize and accept that in every lovingly expressed 'I love you' there was one of our old stories demanding attention and healing. That in every 'I love you' there was the strong hope for love within our own selves. That every 'I love you' challenged us to go beyond our emotional inadequacies and become more loving.

When we marry we want healing

Maybe you like watching sentimental Hollywood movies with a happy ending. Maybe when you opened this book you were hoping for directions to your one and only true love. Maybe you find it very sobering and unromantic when I dissect every 'I love you' as a pathologist dissects lifeless tissue. Maybe you feel deflated by the thought that underneath your little loving iceberg self there is all this struggle and fear. Maybe you're thinking what a spoilsport I am, going on about pain and complicated reopening of old wounds. Maybe you're wondering whether you will have to process your childhood experiences forever, or whether it's your bad, bad parents who are responsible for everything. Maybe you are asking yourself whether it's worth getting involved with someone at all if it's always about needs, wants and repressed fears.

This book is not an attempt to reduce you to a hopeless bunch of walking wounded. It is not about the examination and processing of every minute of your childhood. Quite the opposite. I will prove later, that here, now, today, right under your nose, you have everything you need to heal yourself and your relationship.

It is crucially important both for us personally and for our relationships to know that we all have repressed pain and less attractive parts, and that they all have an impact on our life here and now. But I don't want to suggest that you embark on lifelong self-analysis. All you need do is look at yourself and your relationships with other people in a completely different, maybe even revolutionary way. There are old undigested stories in all of us that wield their power to this day and shield our lively, fluid being like an invisible suit of armour. It is this armour, and not our partner, that prevents us from being happy. I repeat – because it needs repeating, given that this is such a complete and revolutionary change in our consciousness – that the people around us are only triggers, and the closer they are to us, the more precise triggers they are. But they are also our most devoted servants on the way to healing. They are at our command, so that time and again we can transfer our old patterns onto them, repeat them and thereby realize our deepest wish: to heal our pain.

3

Your partner only plays a role in your script

The true point of a relationship will always be to balance the inner conflicts of both partners. For that reason, being in a relationship is the best thing both can possibly do – regardless of what it is like at the moment. You should be glad that your nearest and dearest presses your buttons so precisely that it sometimes hurts. You might as well be grateful for it, because if you want a fulfilling relationship it is essential to pay attention to those parts in yourself that hurt, are destructive or restrict your room for manoeuvre. You might still resent this idea, but if you wish to find real strength in your relationship then for the time being you have no other choice than to deal with the bottom of the iceberg.

This might appear masochistic, but once you are familiar with it, you'll be fascinated, for in each and every negative, painful and destructive part of yourself there is a fundamental power which can help both yourself and your relationship. It is just waiting to be rediscovered and unleashed.

For that to happen, first of all you need to be willing to be responsible for your fear, your negativity and your pain. This doesn't mean hurling yourself into an abyss of doom and depression, it only means refocusing your attention. In your day-to-day life with your partner, from now on stop focusing on what *they* are doing and concentrate on your own responses to it. Once you have learned how to monitor yourself in this way, you need the courage to be really honest with yourself. So far everybody who has followed this path has been surprised and sometimes frightened by the things going on inside them – all the prejudice, the shame and resentment that has kept them from finding love and happiness. But as soon as you are willing to surrender to your own investigations, something will start to change inside you – very subtly you become gentler and more empathic.

If you are prepared to change in this way and continue with it in your everyday life, you will realize that what initially appears to be a passion-killer will ultimately free the path towards real love. Our iceberg is a great thing to have – it's not some sly monster manipulating us from the depths. It is a treasure chest. In it our whole life is stored – every breath, every emotion, every thought – as if on an unlimited-capacity hard disk. It is our whole being. And we should give it our full attention and our love. We should have the most passionate affair with it that we can possibly imagine. We should have the relationship of our life with it.

We fall in love so that we don't have to love

The iceberg is always working for us, even when our conscious mind doesn't see it like that at all. It is a most divine, precise and ingenious instrument and reaches far beyond anything we can comprehend and initiate with our conscious mind. We think that the little conscious part that is visible above the waterline is our loving self. Here we make decisions, take action, fall in love and apparently yearn to stay with someone until death do us part. But what we are actually doing is completely different. Here, at the tip, we plan how our life *should* be. Here we create strategies to avoid our pain and weakness, but in fact they exclude endless possibilities and real love.

As soon as something becomes uncomfortable, we want to change it. When something hurts, we look for the means to soothe the pain. We always rush away, mostly from ourselves. If we don't feel the way we think we should be feeling, we run off into all kinds of addictions or look for a person who might be able to change things. As soon as life is not the way we think it should be, we immediately start developing strategies to bring about improvement. We want to be richer, more successful, more accepted, more beautiful – but there's no way we're prepared to admit that we feel helpless, inadequate, ugly or wrong.

This mechanism can be detected much more easily in individuals than in couples. The minute a love affair is over or there is a bit of slack time in their life, most singles are already on the lookout for the next relationship. I once had a friend who chatted up a woman every time we went to a bar or restaurant and then handed her his card on leaving. He was always busy either attracting women, fighting for them or grieving for a lost relationship. From the perspective of this book he was primarily distracted from himself and his deep inner loneliness.

But couples too have their avoidance strategies. Out of the fear of a real encounter, of perhaps having to tolerate a certain distance and silence on the path to real closeness, they fill up their private diaries with endless events, and their family life is packed with invitations, meetings with friends, trips out, social commitments and hobbies. Time and again couples have told me that they do a lot together but don't know each other at all. I have met several couples in therapy where one partner has a lover who is part of their circle of friends. When they meet, along with their unsuspecting partners, it's just about some secret touching under the table or in the hall.

Some external commitments can be the result of a deep relationship. When two people gain a great deal of strength from each other, they can actively pass some of it on to others. But for most couples whose diaries are bursting with appointments, it is all about distraction. They twitter and flutter like a mother bird leading possible enemies away from the nest. A busy life not only keeps others away, it also distracts us from what needs our undivided attention – our fear and our pain. That is what we need to understand, to nurture and to learn to love. That is what we have to confront with courage.

'You are so weak'

As I mentioned earlier, this doesn't mean that we have to plunge into an intense therapeutic process. This kind of work very rarely needs a therapist. We don't have to do anything really, nor do we have to change. All that is needed is an inner awareness, a willingness to feel our real feelings in every moment.

When Christina came to me she was busy all the time either helping others or looking after relatives. If in the session I managed to ask how *she* was, tears started to roll. Every time those tears surprised her and every time she was very moved when, for a moment at least, she sensed how she really felt.

She made some jokes about what she called my 'witchcraft', but all that happened was that for a brief moment, in response to a very simple question, she attended to herself.

It is these simple honest questions that take us straight to the heart of the iceberg. I'll describe this transformational process in the second part of this book. For now, just remember that everything that you need to know about yourself, all the pain, all the fear, turns up at exactly the right moment and in exactly the right place for you. All you need to do is remain alert.

Christina, the eternal helper, just needed to stop for a moment and look at her life from a different angle. She needed to ask: 'What does all this tell me about myself?' There were needy people all around her and she was the mother of all mothers. With that little question she might have remembered that she had had to play this motherly role earlier, in her family of origin. She might have recognized that time and again, whether in her own family, with her friends or in her neighbourhood, she had embraced this role. And perhaps she might even have recognized how much she was looking for it and yet how it made her suffer at the same time. She might have realized that sometimes she actually hated it. Maybe in the end she might have felt her own deep neediness, cried all her unshed tears and, with this new awareness, managed to break the cycle.

The more often we stand back and take an honest evaluation of our life, the more quickly we will realize that we are following the same script over and over. I have lived in various countries, for instance, have moved house about two dozen times and have changed jobs and partners numerous times, only to humbly learn this one lesson: no matter where I am, no matter who I am with and what I am doing, my experiences are always dependent on my way of looking at life.

Everybody in this world lives out their own personal script. We can change the location and the actors – partners, jobs and places – but the emotional climate and our way of dealing with life will remain. We change the screens on which our movie is shown, we change the set on which it is filmed, but time and again the scripts have similar plots and the actors play similar roles, because we are the writers and directors of our own movie. But we have usually forgotten that.

If you look at your everyday life you will discover examples of this everywhere. I have a friend, for example, who, when meeting someone new, always asks herself whether they can be trusted. She is worried that they might talk behind her back or find out too much about her.

I once went on holiday with another friend. We just wanted to relax for a few days. But we had hardly entered our hotel room when we began to see things differently. I was on the balcony enjoying the lovely view and the fresh air. She was thinking that the room might be quite noisy at night, as it was close to the restaurant. We moved rooms. Later we went to the sauna. After a long walk in wintry weather I felt really comfortable there, but she left after only a few minutes. Later she explained that she found it quite unhygienic. Hadn't I noticed the smell of the woman next to us? And the unattractive feet of the guy on the bench above? No, I hadn't.

We don't see the world as it is – we see our own view of it. Deep inside the iceberg, in our inner projection room, all our sad old stories are still being played out on an endless loop. But we haven't been to this inner projection room for ages.

Most of us have forgotten that it exists. But there is a small hole in the wall behind us, just as in the cinema. From this tiny hole the film is beamed up to the tip of our iceberg on a giant screen, complete with surround-sound and 3-D vision. It's so perfect that we don't even realize that it is only a movie. And the story is so thrilling that we keep forgetting to eat our popcorn.

In this sense Christina relived time and again – completely unconsciously – the story of her own childhood. In her adult life, as in her childhood, there were both small and big men in her family who needed her help, her nurturing and her attention. She rushed from mission to mission and at the end of the day she was usually so exhausted that she hadn't got the energy to figure out what her own feelings were. Every emergency during her day was real; the increasing neediness of the men around her seemed to require her help alone. When I asked how she was, and thereby found the little hole in the projection room, for a moment her tears brought her out of the movie to the place where the real script was being written. She could then attend to herself and discover her own story, and bit by bit she managed to understand why she was so angry at her husband...

As we watch our movie, at the very moment when things get tense, when it seems that the leading man and lady aren't going to live happily ever after, that's when our partner walks in front of the screen. And before we realize what's happening, our projector makes them the baddie and they get the lead in our unprocessed, never-ending story.

That's what happened to Christina. For a long time she hadn't been able to see her husband as he really was. One day he had walked straight across her screen and since then he had been playing the leading role in her old home movie. Christina complained that he didn't care about anything and never noticed what she really needed – even though from the very first moment he had been the most empathic and understanding man she had ever met.

There was a younger brother in Christina's life who had always been the centre of their mother's attention and love. He had seemed weaker than his older sister and so been continually mothered and nurtured. In the course of time, his big sister had become completely deprived of love and care, but all her attempts to draw attention to herself were in vain. In her, weakness was not accepted. The only thing that attracted her mother's attention and devotion was when she looked after the weak brother too. Thus as a little girl Christina learned the rule that trapped her as a grown woman: she only got attention when she helped men. And in order for her to be able to help men, they had to be weak. But if men are weak, there is no real place for a grown-up woman.

You might say that nobody would imitate childhood scenes like that. You might think that normal healthy people would never suffer from such delusions. You might consider it a miracle if we ever met anyone who would play our old games with us, let alone met them all the time. Well, these emotional dynamics may be unlikely and even unreal, but day in, day out, they dominate our perception. We all create our world in exactly the same way that Christina did. And no matter who turns up in our life, they immediately get slotted into a role in our old familiar film.

In Christina's case this occurred primarily with her husband and their son, but also with the other men, young and old, in her neighbourhood. They all were mothered in an unconscious bid for love and attention. And as we all choose the most comfortable life every time, they gratefully accepted this treatment. So Christina took on the role of nurse, helper and carer in her family. For her, closeness was always linked to incompetence and neediness. But this closeness created dependency, and some tried to escape from it. In time her son became an idle good-for-nothing and her husband withdrew.

Through this behaviour both men became so similar to Christina's brother, her mother's favourite, that for the grown-up Christina they became more and more the object of her powerlessness, anger and resentment. By playing her game they had become exactly what she had never wanted to experience again.

Both Christina's husband and son had great potential and intelligence and would have benefited greatly if Christina had found the courage to be herself and to create her own life. To do this, however, she would have had to take the risk of being loved for her own dreams. But if she had stopped suggesting by her constant mothering that the men were weak, everyone in the family would have grown and moved forward.

At some point during our work Christina realized that she had repeated the same pattern in her own family that she had rejected so strongly in her mother's and that this behaviour had earned her very little attention and acceptance as a woman.

Projection – your partner is what you don't want to be

In Christina's story the past had quite a strong influence over her current relationships. Above all, she repeatedly discovered neediness in people which urgently required her help – an emotional neediness she never had allowed herself to indulge in. Only her occasional tears showed how empty, vulnerable and helpless *she* felt.

Psychologists call these dynamics 'projection'. On our way towards truth it is important to fully comprehend what projections are. The word stems from the Latin *proicere*, which means 'to throw away'. When we project, we throw something away from ourselves and onto another person.

In so doing, we analyze another person instead of ourselves. We say things like 'They need help and attention' or 'They are weak', thereby projecting our own unmet needs for help and attention or our own weaknesses onto the other person. We might say 'They don't care' or 'They're inconsiderate' or 'They're never there,' thereby projecting our own lack of care for ourselves and with it our own inability to care, our own helpless withdrawal and our own separateness onto the other person.

Why do we do this? And how can we do it so accurately without even noticing? The answer is always the same – it's the way the ingenious bottom of our iceberg contributes to the healing of our old wounds. Way back as children we were unable to provide ourselves with fairness, acceptance, attention and healing. Receptive as we were, we simply took everything on board and adapted perfectly to the family system. Sometimes this was so painful that we even banished the experience from our memory.

The reliable iceberg, however, stored all this pain up for us and time and again sends it up in ways which are bearable for us, so that we can use it to our advantage. Sometimes we can't tolerate the truth, though, we can't deal with it or accept it, and so we project it onto others. Then we blame them for things that are rooted in our own pain.

Once we understand that we 'throw away' our hurts in this way, we can consider those who have 'caught' them with curiosity, in a spirit of research and compassion, rather than rejecting them, blaming them, fearing them and judging them. Once we start seeing ourselves in what we reject in our partners we will find what we were unable to see in ourselves – and then healing is possible.

Mirrors – your partner is what you cannot see

Once you engage with this concept, the whole dynamics of a relationship are turned around. The old films from the bottom of the iceberg don't have to be projected to the tip any more. Your relationship with your partner becomes a kind of under-water camera. Whatever you yearn for or stumble over on the surface with your partner shows you the stories hidden away deep down in the bulk of the iceberg. And in time – though you might not be able to imagine it yet – you will delight in everything that comes up between you and your partner and be relieved that it can finally be examined.

Your relationship is like a mirror directly in front of your nose. Wherever you turn, the mirror turns with you. Your relationship always mirrors the part that you cannot see and the place you can't discover yourself. Whatever is happening in your relationship is an expression of your relationship with yourself. Everything is a reflection of your own inner landscape. The people around you act out exactly the qualities you carry hidden inside you. Your most intimate partners as well as your most intimate enemies reflect the core of your being. No one can love you if you haven't loved yourself. And no one can harm you in a way you cannot harm yourself.

We can only dissolve this mirage when we identify those parts of our iceberg that others are acting out for us. Once we have dragged them up into our consciousness, we can understand and finally integrate them – which is always the final step. It is about perceiving that everything we believe is external is in ourselves and thus taking it back. Only then do we finally feel that we have everything that we need for our life and that we are just as complete as anybody else.

The question 'What does it have to do with me?' should be your constant companion in this process. It immediately creates understanding and closeness. And by focusing on integrating all the parts of our personality in every human encounter, we also become more compassionate, flexible and positive. We broaden our understanding and our natural charisma and expand our control over our life.

Shadows – your partner is what you don't like

Neediness, pain and inadequacy are the issues in sentimental early evening soaps. But deep down, in the projection room of our iceberg, there are late-night movies featuring really evil villains. Villains are not very popular, but in every really enthralling thriller they have a main role. Can you think of somebody in your life you really don't like, someone you condemn or even hate? Somebody who was really once quite close to you but who has cheated on you, humiliated you or abused you? This person is your shadow. They represent a completely isolated part of your iceberg hulk – an aspect of your self-rejection and your self-hate. They show you something that you condemn yourself for.

What can it possibly have to do with us when other people do things that hurt us? When our partner is hardly ever at home, cheats on us, treats the children badly or is always emotionally blackmailing us? When our boss humiliates us in front of everybody, exploits our goodwill, takes away our power and replaces us with someone else? Or when we have to take a particularly inconsiderate and stubborn adversary to court? All this immediately triggers anger, pain, helplessness, guilt and fear in us. But often we hide away from the destructive self-hate reflected by those conflicts.

Dealing with the shadow requires a lot of courage and honesty. But once we are willing to look at it more closely, we will always be able to identify it. It is exactly the opposite of what we'd like to be, what we believe ourselves to be or what corresponds to our role in our family or society. Sometimes, in particularly clear moments, we recognize, when dealing with the shadow, that we are envious or jealous or lacking exactly what the representative of our shadow owns. But such insights are rare exceptions. Mostly we reject the shadow categorically and are trapped in a complete polarization: either our shadow has power, success, freedom and influence or it has compassion, care, justice and honourable intentions. And if our shadow has one, we will feel linked to the other.

Every person has a shadow. And shadows always turn up where things are moving in an extreme direction. The more at ease we feel, the more extreme adversaries will turn up in our life and the more frequently and intensely we will have to deal with those we detest so much – feminists and traditionalists, blacks and whites, Christians and Muslims, nuclear protestors and nuclear advocates, stern parents and rebellious children, divorcees and their ex-partners. Once the willingness to communicate grows, however, the boundaries become softer and more vague. If the split is cemented further, on the other hand, the power struggle becomes more intense.

Often we can watch these dynamics at work during a separation. Two people who once got together and married in the spirit of true love eventually get divorced and embark on bitter warfare.

The fallen angel

What is it, down there in our iceberg hulk, that we detest so much that we hide it away and never connect it to ourselves? Very early in life we probably did something that caused pain either to ourselves or others. It is likely that we were actually just doing something when something bad happened, and so we unconsciously formed a link between the two. As I said before, children don't have a clear boundary between themselves and what is happening around them. So maybe we were absorbed in a wonderfully engrossing game when one of our siblings had an accident. Then maybe a parent said something like 'You should have looked out for them.' And so inside us a link was formed that said: 'Whenever I play happily and am carefree, something terrible happens.' After that we thought the carefree part of ourselves was 'bad' and banned it from our consciousness. And later in life we found ourselves reacting overcautiously and responsibly and condemning carefree, jolly people as irresponsible.

Often a particularly pervasive atmosphere in families or societies has a severe impact on a child's development. This could be the degenerative disease of a parent, constant arguments leading to divorce, an imbalance of power between the parents, strict rules, ethnic persecution or narrow religious and moral boundaries. In such an atmosphere things that are completely normal for children will be condemned as 'bad' or 'evil'. Nakedness, for instance, will be held to be a sin and physical exuberance immoral. A neighbour's children of a different skin colour or religion will be arch-enemies, and being noisy will make Daddy ill.

It's equally repressive for a child to have to choose between Mummy and Daddy, between the weaker and the stronger parent. Children want to love everybody in the same way, at all costs. But if they are forced to make a decision, either because of arguments, separation or the weakness of a parent, then they have to split part of themselves off. The part which still loves the other parent is 'bad' and not allowed to exist any longer, even though the parent might have left the family or want to leave, or might shout at Daddy or beat Mummy up.

Extremely strict rules and prohibitions in a family also contribute significantly to the forming of a shadow. The child tries to act within those boundaries and behave correctly, but in spite of its best efforts, its natural strengths and desires will rise to the surface and then have to be pushed back down into the 'bad' forbidden realm of the shadow. Later in life, when all those natural desires surface again, they are distorted and disfigured as greed, hate, revenge, gluttony or promiscuity. Sometimes they lead us to live a virtually double life.

While I was writing this book, the name Michael Friedmann made headlines. Friedmann was a public institution in Germany – the vice-president of the Central Council of the Jews in Germany, a lawyer, a member of the Conservative party and a media personality – and he claimed a particularly high moral and political ground, always aiming for the highest standards in justice, religion, morals, retribution and credibility.

With so much emphasis – and in his case public emphasis – on virtue and responsibility, it's easy for life to get out of kilter. Such inner demands put pressure on people and this causes a constant inner imbalance. After a while all the forbidden desires build up and break through particularly forcefully. In fact this apparently incorruptible high priest of honesty was accused of drug misuse, sexual excesses with prostitutes and having contacts in the underworld. One of the prosecutors declared that the Friedmann case would keep the tabloids happy for several weeks.

From this book's perspective, Friedmann had an entire 'shadow cabinet'. The faultless public image he had created as a kind of chief moral inquisitor meant that unconsciously he was forced to permanently judge himself according to his exaggerated standards. No space was left for the human weaknesses and fallibility from which vitality and compassion can arise. His desire for immediate, authentic physical contact was also obviously huge. But his natural physical impulses were not allowed to unfold freely. It seems that he had dissociated himself from their unruly power so strongly that eventually he could only overcome this rift by taking drugs. Only under their mind-expanding influence was he able to connect with his physical self – but still not in an authentic way, only via excessive promiscuity in a secret underworld distorted by drugs.

Michael Friedmann's future won't be easy. But if he faces it with courage and confronts his true self, then he could emerge from this crisis with a real strength and vitality which could move the hearts of a society for which so far he has only functioned as a paragon of virtue.

Friedman wanted to do the right thing, but he took it all too far. This phenomenon can be observed with many celebrities and politicians. Increased power and public exposure don't often go hand-in-hand with increased personal growth, authenticity and integrity.

'Integrity' is a word often used in political and economic contexts. If you want to live a life of integrity, of real personal fulfilment and honest expression, if you want to touch people with your heart and soul, then you will not be able to get away with integrating your unconscious parts little by little. A shadow which has not been integrated back into the personality will have a profound effect, and this is particularly noticeable in public roles. In this sense, when choosing the right candidate for public office, it is important to focus on the person's character rather than experience.

'I've become just as thoughtless as my husband!'

In a relationship we very often aim to change our partner. Their otherness unconsciously reminds us of our old pain and guilt. Consequently we try to get them to see, do or feel things the way we do. I could list you at least a dozen qualities of my husband's that I once considered good reasons for a divorce. But today I see them as important impulses for my own personal development and growth.

One of the most beautiful ways to fill your marriage with strength and life is to recognize the otherness of your partner as your own biggest desire. I am only able to write this book today because I now allow myself to have qualities that for a time I angrily rejected in my husband. I am only able to write these pages because I am *irresponsible* and *reckless*, don't care about *security*, have *no serious interest in the wellbeing of my family* and what they think of me and have *selfishly* withdrawn from everything and *recklessly* transferred all responsibility for our family life to my husband.

Of course I am not really advocating inconsiderateness, recklessness or irresponsibility. It is not about becoming the way we thought the shadow once was (and maybe really was), but about adding something to our own being.

In the darkest hours of our marriage my husband really was hardly more than a rare guest in our family hotel and never asked me what I thought about his withdrawal and his life without us. I was a mother hen and a kind of sergeant major of the household. He was only half there – but so was I. I lacked what he had. He lacked what made my life worth living. Today I can make use of his clear boundaries for things that are beneficial for both of us. And at home he is now present with his light-hearted and carefree ways, so that our life in general has become much more relaxed and fun.

A wicked mother-in-law can be our closest ally

Our family members very often act out the most important parts we have disconnected from so that we can integrate them and heal. Our parents, our siblings and later our partner and children all represent parts of ourselves that we simply have to own again. 'But some things are unforgivable,' I hear you say. 'The story of your husband and his recklessness is just a harmless example. After all, there are women who cheat on their husbands with his best mate. There are men who desert their wives and children. There are wicked mothers-in-law, neglectful mothers and fathers who beat up their children. And we should try and own some of *that*?'

I could quote dozens of similar examples, but would prefer to suggest that it's better not to dwell on the most despicable behaviour. That will only distract you from what this is really about – your life and your relationship.

So I am asking you now to look at the person who at this very moment triggers the hottest anger in you, someone you find absolutely detestable and really want to get out of your life. Now have the courage to ask yourself honestly: 'What do they have in their life that I would like to have? What do they allow themselves that I would not allow myself? What are they free of that I am trapped by?' If you are really truthful, you'll discover one of your biggest desires in the answer, and one of your greatest talents, something that you once had and at some point experienced as bad or painful, something that you were never allowed to develop in your family.

When we look honestly at our shadow, we not only discover our greatest loss but also something that our whole family of origin was lacking. Whether it is light-heartedness, courage, a fighting spirit or the ability to create wealth, whether it is playfulness, the seeking of physical pleasure, earthiness or an unquenchably free spirit, no matter what quality our shadow represents in reality, let's finally take it back, let's give it space in our life and then we will gain a strength that will not only benefit us but also our whole family of origin.

Our iceberg continually challenges us to grow and develop. If we courageously dive down to its depths, we not only find our so-called evil villains, but also painful lessons that our family hasn't learned for generations. Let's reclaim the lost parts of ourselves, let's grow up and then we can give our own family what we never received. You have no idea how liberating this can be. And you have no idea how overwhelming your feelings will be once you have made peace with your shadow.

When the iceberg melts...

When we attend to the deep hulk of our iceberg and recognize its infinite diversity and potential, every relationship with another person suddenly offers a path to discovery and self-development. I have only outlined a few possibilities here with the inner child, the projection, the mirror, the shadow and the old family patterns. There are numerous other strategies and processes within our iceberg that have not been mentioned. It is not that important to know every one of them.

If all this has given you the impression that you will be facing an entire lifetime of self-analysis, or that you will now have to view your whole childhood as a tragedy and your parents as abusers, don't despair. If my stories and their sometimes complex implications have confused you, or you couldn't follow them, it doesn't matter! I haven't told you all this in order to make you analyze every aspect of your childhood. I would simply like to motivate you to become present in your life again. There's no need to undergo an agonizing analysis of the past – every moment of the present will show you what to do, as long as you are willing to really be yourself again.

In this chapter I intended first and foremost to induce something in your consciousness to change. That's why I explained everything to your conscious mind. You don't need the details, but your conscious mind needs a fundamental understanding of the processes within the iceberg, otherwise it will perpetually undermine your path towards compassion, closeness and love in your relationship with doubts and intellectual arguments.

It will be enough if I have been able to communicate just one message in this chapter, namely that your partner may not be responsible for your sad, lonely, cut-off, helpless and maybe even hateful feelings. This insight alone, without any understanding of the psychological details involved, is enough to revive your relationship. Even if you can only half-understand it, your relationship can benefit from new hope and strength, and you can become softer and more open.

I haven't only seen these emotional dynamics with the people who have come to me as clients. I have also experienced the same thing with my husband, and for that I am infinitely grateful. I have been able to open up to the real intention of my unconscious mind and have learned that all his strategies, all his stubbornness only served one purpose – to heal our old wounds and to connect us so closely that our icebergs could melt. Whenever in the course of our life and our marriage we have embraced and warmed our icebergs with our consciousness and love, parts of them have dissolved and become part of the ocean. And that is their real goal.

4

The more in love, the harder the fall

If our relationship is the most wonderful place for personal growth and healing, if we understand it as the university where we can take a degree in maturity, then it makes sense that the course follows certain steps, each of them with a specific task. If, however, we don't recognize and understand those steps, those new tasks and ever-increasing challenges, then very soon they will appear to be huge obstacles.

As soon as the first rush of love fades or our relationship seems to go off the boil we feel a failure. We badly miss the good feelings. And instead we are either confronted by emptiness or entangled in a struggle.

At the very point when, in my opinion, the real adventure of a relationship starts – when all the old wounds and scars are beginning to show, when the masks come down, when two people meet in naked truthfulness and acceptance, when it's possible to lose yourself and heal – it's often the very beginning of the end. There is a dawning realization that we won't get what we want and we withdraw into mute disappointment. We yearn for passion, but bad habits sneak in. We compare our relationship to that of other couples, and realize that it is totally different. Wistfully we remember our old romance and have to acknowledge that it has evaporated.

Relationships are always in flux. They bob us up and down like waves on the ocean. Sometimes we get dragged under and it seems that we are slowly being pulled further away from our partner. Sometimes it appears that our relationship is slowly but inevitably trundling into a cul-de-sac from which we can only be saved by separation.

If, however, we understand the steps of development inherent in every relationship and we know which point of our journey we are at, we can develop a new and reassuring perspective. If there are maelstroms in the natural flow of our relationship, it doesn't mean that something is wrong with it, with our partner or with ourselves. In fact, the demands to heal, to integrate unconscious aspects of ourselves and to accept the otherness of our partner *increase* with every phase. Each phase offers its own opportunities. Each phase has its own challenges. If we really understand this in our heart then it can be fine just to change nappies or to pursue our career single-mindedly for a while. It might even make sense not to feel like having sex for a time. It can be liberating to be angry and quarrelsome now and then. And it can even be understandable to need more distance from our partner once in a while.

If we accept that things change, we can move forward as a couple and our love can deepen. This can happen even if only one of us is willing to consider the emerging tasks as opportunities for learning.

The phases of a relationship are built upon each other. Only when each one has been managed and understood can the relationship move on to the next one. I learned this model from the American relationship specialist Chuck Spezzano. Initially it made my own marriage much easier. Later I passed it on to countless clients. From this perspective, the relationship processes suddenly make sense. Developments which appear to be a dead end become meaningful. Painful phases turn out to be not the road to divorce but opportunities for growth and development.

The romantic rush

Most relationships begin with romance. We feel giddy and light-hearted, are constantly yearning for our partner and long to be close to them. We indulge each other, surprise each other with gestures large and small, write love letters and poems, give each other flowers and hide little messages under the pillow or by the toothbrush. Not even in our wildest dreams can we imagine ever experiencing anything negative with this wonderful person. They seem perfect, and when we are together we feel perfect too.

For a long time each of our cells has yearned to feel this way –whole at last. For a long time we have looked for someone who could accept us completely. For a long time we have hungered for confirmation that we are special. On the whole, much of this phase is about feeling special. When everything is new and we don't know this intriguing stranger very well, we tell our friends that we have met a very special person – one who treats *us* as a very special person, one who looks, thinks and acts in very special ways, one who emanates something totally special. One who loves us in a very special way. Filled with romantic ideas, we actually believe that this person is capable of making us feel whole again. We are 100 per cent convinced that they are our missing half, and that is why we enter into a relationship with them.

At this point we are at the heart of a seemingly perfect romantic illusion. A woman experienced in all aspects of love once said to me that during this phase nobody should be allowed to sign contracts or to make important professional or personal decisions. She was convinced that people in love were in an exceptional state of intoxication, cut off from reality.

What drives us into a relationship is the hope of becoming whole again. It is this feeling of completeness that invariably makes us happy in life. When we are in love, we are immersed in the illusion that this feeling is only due to the other person. In reality, this is *never* the case.

In spite of this, this in-love phase gives us something wonderful and important – it enables us to enter into a relationship with another person. It is essential for exactly this reason. It brings the two of us together and gives us a hint of something better than the loneliness and separateness that we have become used to. It gives us hope that our longing for wholeness can actually be fulfilled.

The romantic phase of love appears to be the perfect relationship. It gives us a feeling of warmth and closeness. We are constantly fantasizing about that wonderful other person – and that makes us feel good. But all this longing and fantasizing is not about our partner. At this point we really have no idea of what they are like. Very likely we perceive them through a haze. Many of the exciting feelings and fantasies are nothing but projections from inside ourselves. But still the phase of being in love shows us how many wonderful things we might experience if we truly manage to transform our relationship into something else. If we are ready to give our love. If we are ready to accept this person just as they are and not as we have imagined them. If we are ready to heal together.

For that reason, we should fully enjoy the phase of being in love. We need the memory of its uplifting power in order to get through more difficult phases later. When we wake up from our intoxication and find ourselves in a less pleasant reality, when the other person doesn't fit our ideal image but turns out to be just themselves, we can look back, full of nostalgia but also with hope. Such memories can even be vital to our survival as a couple, for those moments when we end up asking ourselves, full of doubt: 'Are they really the right partner for me?'

At those times of crisis when the option of separation is just around the corner, everybody should remember one thing: that first rush of love, with all its possibilities, shows the true potential of a relationship. And it can all come back again, bit by bit, even after decades, once the two people involved are on their way to healing. The second time around it will have a different kind of depth and truthfulness. However, in most cases the path that leads there is long and winding and runs through much less peaceful terrain.

Sobering up in a power struggle

After such an intense romantic intoxication and so many high hopes, sobering up is inevitable. As with all toxic substances, the more often and intensely we fall in love, the quicker the high subsides, the harder we fall and the stronger the next shot has to be. In the case of relationships, the come-down leads directly into a power struggle.

All our yearnings during the in-love phase have only one aim: to get closer to the new partner and to intensify this closeness. So we can't actually avoid getting to know them better – which inevitably triggers the realization that they aren't that perfect after all.

The most extreme story I have heard about this phase is Dora's. Dora came to me feeling totally drained and disillusioned by her marriage. Tears streaming down her face, she told me that her husband had been her dream man and that initially she had felt very special to him. Her voice then became hard and cold and she told me how she had lost all respect for him and how boring and weak she found him now. She said he had become more and more inattentive, and untidy, and she wasn't turned on by him at all and could hardly bear to lie next to him at night. Recently she had had quite a few affairs – well, not even affairs, just one-night stands – and now she wanted to split up with him, because she had had a magical experience with someone else. When she recalled this, Dora's face lit up.

Dora had brought a stack of letters and tapes with her. They were all from a man she had met in a café only a few hours before he was due to travel back to Australia, his home country. She had spent an afternoon with him, just talking and talking... That afternoon her heart had opened up. Nothing physical had happened, but she had met a soul mate. From that day on, the two had sent each other countless e-mails and tapes and had posted imaginative presents halfway across the globe. It was as if Dora had collected extensive evidence of a most romantic love story.

What she had come to me for was advice on achieving a fair and amicable separation from her husband. It would have to be quick as well, because her adored correspondent was going to come over in a few months. By that time she wanted to have clarity for everybody involved and to have laid the foundation for her new wonderful love.

Dora was a successful businesswoman, used to acting decisively once she had made her mind up. And her mind *was* made up about her love for the stranger. She told me she felt changed by him. Never before had she felt so close to someone in so many ways. She was full of passion and tenderness, they would be inspirational for each other professionally, and – well, she had even started swinging her hips again...

My attempts to achieve a satisfying resolution between Dora and her husband all failed. We had a few talks together during which Dora was bitter and monosyllabic, almost shy. When she came to see me on her own, she still appeared intoxicated by thoughts of her intended. And she was working purposefully for the dissolution of her marriage – and for Day X.

To cut a long story short, Day X was a few weeks later. After months of waiting Dora picked up her dream lover, now a real person, from the airport and spent two days with him. Then she came to me, crying her eyes out. This was not the man of the letters, she sobbed. This man was petty, inflexible and quite highly strung. He even looked different from how she had remembered him. He was the biggest disappointment of her life...

The closer we get to another person, the more clearly we see their faults – or, to be honest, how they really are. And all the aspects that we were so magically attracted to before turn out to be differences that separate us. The person who initially brought so much joy and light-heartedness into our life on closer inspection turns out to be unreliable. He comes home late, lets us wait, has fun with other people. The passionate creature who made our life so vibrant now tends to make quite violent scenes and create a lot of drama. The solid rock turns out to be petty and rigid. The erotic aura of our new lover comes across as quite vulgar when we see them with our family. The down-to-earth solid person is really quite simple and unimaginative in everyday life...

All sorts of things don't meet our expectations. All sorts of expectations are not met. And because this person is the chosen one, those things hurt, the pain is deep and the faults weigh particularly heavily. And if the person doesn't fly back to Australia, never to be seen again, but shares our house and home, we will find that the distance between us is still as wide as if they were in Australia.

Under no circumstances can we leave the doors to our heart so wide open. We get wary, take precautions. For fear of further hurt we fend off further intimacy.

Everything that we had hoped would be a calm source of fulfilment has to be fought for now. And amid the emotional pushing and pulling, the quarrel about expectations begins. At this point we seem to get less and less of what we liked about the other person, but we want more and more of it. We want to change what's happening, to repress or to stave off the pain and hurt.

Both partners fight with different means, but it is always a bit like a dance – back and forth. One partner tidies the house more and more meticulously while the other makes a mess and behaves more and more thoughtlessly. One comes home later and later while the other pushes for more help at home. One starts more and more fundamental discussions while the other becomes less talkative. One demands more and more sex while the other wants it less and less...

A power struggle is not only a fight to meet our own needs. It can also be a withdrawal from the other person's pressures and expectations. Whether through a compulsive need for order and closeness, a helpless withdrawal through chaos and absence, physical denial or sexual greed, both partners are trying to protect and hide their old fears and wounds as well as they can, while outwardly they are fighting to preserve their ideal of a relationship, life and the partner or to manipulate the other person into following their example.

Hardly anybody wins in this struggle. Instead, the positions just get more entrenched. While one partner nags more and more, the other one distances themselves even further. And that unique 'other half', once so special and perfect, turns into someone we either wish to defeat or to run away from, because they are the person who can hurt us most.

Sometimes in this power-struggle phase we don't even recognize ourselves. Deeply disappointed, we say worse things about our lover than about our worst enemy. Whilst before we told all our friends how wonderful and perfect they were, now we whinge about their incredible thoughtlessness. Sometimes we get really frightened by how much anger and resentment we are directing against them. We are confused and appalled that we can feel such unbelievable resentment and contempt for someone, sometimes after a very short time. These feelings are just as intense as our former adoration. Eventually we feel betrayed by our partner and blame ourselves for not checking them out properly or accuse them of having manipulated us.

Many couples separate during this phase. And even more people find themselves in exactly the same situation, only with a new partner. 'This is not the right one either!' they sigh with resignation, without understanding the process from infatuation to reality and eventually to power struggle. They have no idea how many opportunities to develop and heal their own selves are hidden in that relationship, no inkling that another person is offering them the chance to grow beyond their own limitations.

'Lone wolf' and 'cling-on'

Once you have survived the power struggle without separating, but probably without having really understood it, you'll promptly stumble into the next trap: dependency.

By now both partners are slowly coming to terms with the fact that nothing is as ideal, as vibrant and as fluid as they had thought at the beginning. They keep a bit more distance from each other and start to settle into their opposite roles, to entrench their positions. Both, in their own ways, fight for the least vulnerable and safest position – one that is rather distanced and independent while being as successful, as absent, as indispensable, as accepted and as desirable as possible. After all the power struggles, it feels like a holiday.

Most of the time the power-struggle phase ends with a stubborn fight for this kind of independence. After all the disappointments and hurts, it seems finally possible to regain a bit of control over our life. We can either make our partner do things our own way or, if this does not work, we can simply withdraw and stop playing the game.

Of course, on a deeper level this phase of the relationship is again about balancing out the inner conflicts of both partners. That is why things are linked now too. As soon as one person has moved far enough into the seemingly safe independent position, the other one inevitably finds themselves in the role of dependency. 'I don't want to today ... I can't tomorrow ... I don't know ... I have to go...' leads to 'Please come home, can't you be more attentive, and why don't you do things with the kids...?'

During the phase of infatuation our lives were fused together symbiotically. This apparent closeness now turns into a confusing feeling of 'dis-appointment' and being chained up. Both partners became entangled in the chaos of the power struggle where there are rarely true winners. That is why the relationship then polarizes. The more one closes up and stops responding, the more intensely the other has to try and reach out. This role-play is mutually dependent, but the partners can take turns in the course of a relationship. Tom, for example, had to fight hard to win Tina. Because she was so attractive, during the first few years of their marriage he was very jealous. Then Tina had a baby and was instantly thrown into dependency. Now she waits impatiently for Tom to come home and accuses him of being married to his job. That will only change again when she goes back to work and enjoys some success.

From the outside it might look as though one person is in a worse position than the other in this game of dependency. In reality, the seemingly independent 'lone wolf' is in at least as dissatisfying a position as the dependent 'cling-on'. The partner who withdraws is likely to do it unconsciously to avoid their vulnerability and unprocessed fear of rejection and neediness. Not infrequently 'lone wolves' turn out to be sensitive souls, hungry for love. And quite often the whinge-ing 'cling-ons' secretly dream of popping out to the shops and never coming back.

Roles like that form a vicious circle. One partner remains uninvolved, doesn't want to move in together, marry, plan a holiday, do Christmas together or share other important rituals. They can neither take on everyday responsibilities nor show their love by words or gestures. They prevent this unconsciously, out of fear of loss and rejection, as well as fear of feeling needy. They don't *want* to need anything and withdraw to the independent position, saying: 'Well, maybe...'

This, however, makes the other partner feel disappointed and insecure, and they respond by clinging and nagging – that is, with exactly the neediness and vulnerability that the seemingly independent one wanted to avoid. In a strange way – and a very accurate way – this unconsciously reminds the independent one of their own fears and makes them withdraw even further. The apparently dependent one, of course, promptly responds with even more whingeing and clinging. But they too are only seemingly committed. In a certain way they are using the other one to fill their gaps and as a source of fulfilment. It looks as if they are concerned with closeness and the expression of feelings, but on a deeper level they aren't giving freely either. They might be more present physically, but inwardly they too are not really prepared to give, or capable of it, and they too are driven by fear.

In this phase, each partner actually displays the hurt and pain of the other. Whatever one keeps hidden, the other acts out. So things can easily get out of kilter. If the eternal bachelor eventually decides to propose, the pining lady is suddenly swamped by doubts. If the cling-on stops being available full-time, the lone wolf is suddenly driven by jealousy and swears eternal love. If in one relationship we have been driven to the end of our tether by our partner's clinging, in the next one we'll suddenly find ourselves a virtual barnacle. And this to and fro is never about love but always about control.

We find this inevitable polarization in all areas of relationships. The closer we get to each other, the more we have to acknowledge that we see the world from different angles. One person looks at it through rose-tinted spectacles while the other feels blue. We all know couples where one is optimistic, idealistic and enthusiastic and the other pedantic and conscientious. And while they themselves may be engaged in endless battles about right or wrong, outside observers have no trouble in recognizing that both approaches are necessary for success.

In this phase the partners may paralyze each other with endless discussions about life that only serve to further entrench their positions, even though if they were to co-operate and appreciate each other's capabilities, both would reach their goal. The truth is, again, that it is the very characteristics, perspectives, world views and ways in which we are attacking each other that we should be integrating into our own life to make it richer. If you don't want to be sitting at home waiting, go out. If you are afraid of too much closeness, say what you feel.

The ice age

If all the polarization makes you feel stuck, if it's a complete stalemate, if independence isn't leading to anything but loneliness, then slowly but surely a leaden heaviness will penetrate the relationship. At some point you might well think: 'We are only together because of the children/because we've been married so long/because of our debts/our parents...' It is as if the relationship only exists because of external commitments and inside it is completely empty. After all the power struggles and the battles over right and wrong, after the constant shifting between dependence and independence, all life in the relationship seems to have been paralyzed. Boredom seeps in, being together feels like being in a cage. We fill our day with routines and ask ourselves whether this is really all there is. Any relationship seems to be better than ours. We are a couple – frighteningly, inevitably a couple – but we lack any instinctive, powerful, inner connectedness. We have an uneasy sense that our relationship is coming to an end. We know that we can't go on like this, because we will shrivel up and die.

Roger had been married for a long time. He had a family and was a successful businessman, travelled a lot and held a string of voluntary positions. He had always had a precise idea of what his life should be like. His home was very presentable, his wife the perfect hostess. As she had a good ear for languages, she accompanied him on all his business trips and danced perfectly with him at all the charity balls. But at home, they hardly talked to each other. They slept in separate bedrooms and ate different food. By now Roger had a secret love child by one of his employees. They had taken drugs together and shared a love for Latin dance clubs, 'bottom touching included', as Roger described it.

Such an ice age in a relationship is always the result of inner withdrawal and external role-playing. Both partners are only present in their roles – they function as a marriage partner/parent/provider/hostess/public companion, but as people they are not connected any more. In some Mediterranean carnival processions there are huge papier-mâché figures hiding a normal-sized person who is carrying the contraption. After a certain period of marriage, we often function like those people carrying huge papier-mâché figures around.

Often at some point during our marriage something has hurt us but we haven't had the courage to explain it to our partner and so there has been no hope of healing the wound together. Maybe we were jealous or we felt humiliated but never admitted to it. Maybe we withdrew step by step because we couldn't share something important with our partner. Sometimes I see women who have started faking orgasms and then not been able to stop afterwards. Over the years, behind the mask of the passionate lover, they have felt increasing loneliness and emptiness, but they have kept their anger and resentment hidden from the one who is supposed to give them satisfaction.

Sometimes, as a means of revenge, we deliberately deny ourselves and starve ourselves. Sometimes we feel guilty because in some areas we don't feel close to our partner any more. Those dynamics have an extreme impact on our sex life. In everyday life there is no discussion of how we really feel and neither of us knows where the other is at. All inner-connectedness disappears from the relationship. It dries out. But neither of the partners admits this truthfully. Maybe neither is really conscious of it. At some point one of them loses all desire for sex. But because they cannot link this to the lack of emotional closeness between them, they feel guilty and don't understand their withdrawal.

In order to avoid this frozen emptiness in which the natural, mature closeness to another person has been lost, many people look for a symbiotic replacement. In this process, like mother and child in the early years, we fuse with each other. The voice goes up an octave when Honey talks to Pet, or Sweety is happy when Eeyore comes home. Our boundaries are blurred, we are no longer two individuals but feel connected to our partner by a rubber band. When they move, we are forced to move too. Unconsciously we feel dependent all the time, but hide our fear of showing our true feelings behind a childlike friendliness. But true connectedness is based on real attraction and freedom. Then we simply want to be with each other and feel in touch consistently. Symbiotic fusion, in contrast, blurs the contours of our personality, allows only childlike friendliness and leads to self-sacrifice and dependency.

When real contact between the partners is disturbed or lost, we often start to play compensatory roles in order not to endanger the relationship. We learned to do this in early childhood so that we would be accepted by our family. Countless times we more or less voluntarily surrendered our vitality and spontaneity to either the open or unspoken demands of our family. But every time a part of our real life force froze. Then later, in our relationships, we turned into dutiful housewives and reliable providers, but felt empty inside and wondered why.

We do the right thing and care for our families. But we do it for the wrong reasons – mechanically, without inner motivation from the heart. In fact the less alive and connected we feel from the heart, the more perfectly we play our roles and the larger the papier-mâché figures that we carry around. And, trapped inside them as we are, the less we can be reached by other people. We sacrifice ourselves for our idea of a relationship rather than have immediate contact with another person.

It might sound absurd, but the less fulfilment we get from these roles, the more we perfect them. Over time we trust ourselves less and less to show who we really are. And because we feel less and less acceptable, loveable and desirable inside, we control ourselves more and more, while behind the façade we get increasingly angry, bitter, disappointed and irritable. At some point we turn into a time bomb ready to explode, but often we distract ourselves so much with addictions and activities that eventually we hide our sad explosive confusion from ourselves as well.

In order to keep on functioning under all this inner pressure, we add rules to our roles. We work out how we ought to behave, and we do so. Consciously or unconsciously, we compensate for all our feelings of guilt, failure and separateness by behaving particularly well. We sacrifice ourselves. But all those new rules only have one purpose: to protect us from further pain and prevent others from taking control away from us. In fact the rules that are supposed to save us make our life unbearably empty, frozen and lifeless. They ensure that we no longer have meaningful contact with anybody.

Some people start every sentence with 'one' followed by an auxiliary verb: 'One should, one ought, one must, if one...' That was the case with Howard. Every time he greeted me, it was with a fixed smile and an elaborate compliment. Then he sat down and talked of what 'one' should do. For a long time it remained impossible to coax an 'I will' or 'I want' from him. In the same way, every attempt to actually get closer to him failed. If for a moment I succeeded in reaching his heart, Howard simply beamed at me and began to describe how things were supposed to be. His wife had left him and had cut him out of her life with a frightening coldness and bitterness. She refused to have even a single meeting with him. When I finally met her, she looked like someone whose soul had been cut with shards of glass.

At this stage of a relationship we function in an exemplary way, but we don't give anything of ourselves and avoid any contact with our inner self because we primarily feel anger, resentment, helplessness, pain and guilt. Beneath this explosive mixture is our deepest, most loveable being. But we have no contact any more with its nurturing influence, and accordingly our contact to the outside world is functionally cold, mechanically exemplary but in the end dried up and feeble.

Again we are in a vicious circle. Again it is rooted in the patterns of our childhood. And again it is important to get in touch with our inner self and our real truth. We have to use this ice age to melt away all our old hurts, rather than compensate for them by behaving well but without any spark of real life. This frozen and empty wasteland may seem to be the end of the relationship, but it harbours the possibility of the most profound healing.

'You make me sick'

If even the paralysis and the leaden heaviness have neither brought about more awareness and healing nor led to a separation, if we carry on wearing our masks, then it can lead to illness and death. When all our symbiotic fusion, all our self-sacrificing friendliness, all our rules and roles, all our power struggles and other battles have not brought about the attention and care our heart is yearning for, then unconsciously we only have one option: we have to get ill.

'*Have* to get ill' – maybe you think that is taking it too far. How can you *make* yourself ill? I could write a whole book about the link between body and soul, and there are many books about it already. Our body is our helper, our executive organ. It is the place where our unconscious thoughts and needs, our real truth, show through. It is the place where we can recognize how deeply divided we are inside. It is the place where our will, our discipline and our ideals are defeated by our addictions. It is the place where many things happen that are disliked by our conscious mind. We want to be faithful, but every fibre of our body desires someone else. We want to be slim, but our body puts on weight. We smile happily and openly, but cross our arms over our chest. We don't set boundaries with other people, but get a cold sore on our lips.

We recognize quite early in life that the unconscious interaction between mind and body can be an advantage. Many children realize quickly that an illness brings a lot of attention from their parents, that Mum and Dad indulge them then with the kind of care that they don't get at any other time. On a deeper level we learn early that our sick body helps us to get something that our mind craves.

In this context illness also has a secondary advantage. Consciously we call for the doctor, for medicine, for healing, but unconsciously we don't really want to be well, healthy, strong and fit, because that includes the risk of not being held and taken care of.

That is why later in life we so often find illness on the battle-ground of love. One of the partners is weak and delicate – and has frequently been sick quite often earlier in the relationship – and when the relationship becomes increasingly lifeless, they get so ill that the other person is simply forced to give them love, care and attention. I believe there are countless cases in which one person, after years of loneliness and coldness in the marriage, has simply resorted to becoming seriously ill.

I know a woman who over a period of more than 20 years sank deeper and deeper into depression and eventually could only function with the help of medication and regular stays in a psychiatric clinic. On a practical day-to-day level her husband organized everything, and the worse she became, the more perfectly he did it. But he had long ceased to be able to give her the emotional attention she was craving. After years of increasing mental and physical illness on her part and better-organized services on his, he finally found another relationship and managed to separate from his wife, despite huge feelings of guilt on his side and threats of suicide on hers. Then, as the target for her attention-seeking behaviour had left, the woman's illness lost its deeper meaning – and in less than a year after the separation she was well again.

There is yet another aspect of illness and love: the self-sacrifice. A partner in this role is always busy, works hard, doesn't look after themselves and their weaknesses, often indulges in one or more addictions and heroically ignores every sign of a possible illness. While this is not immediately recognizable, this person too is desperately calling for care and attention. Unconsciously they are neglecting themselves in the hope of finding someone who will look after them and love them more than they love themselves. Of course, they would never admit to this, and would never ask for it either. Quite the opposite – if someone like that were to turn up in their life, they would stubbornly refuse all advice and help. I know couples where the wife has developed into the perfect nurse and therapist, only to watch helplessly as the husband withdraws more and more, works harder and harder, smokes and drinks more and more, has an increasingly unhealthy diet and develops more and more symptoms of illness.

Whether through illness or self-sacrifice, relationships shaped by this pattern are a good illustration of the fact that every couple is a system with unconscious dynamics at play. Behind illness and self-sacrifice are fear, self-rejection and the wish – maybe even a subtle struggle – for acceptance. But, of course, trying to gain the love and attention of our partner in this way never works, because it results in a business relationship without any voluntary giving. And voluntary giving is *the* necessary condition for healing in every relationship.

It never stops – but it does get better

All these phases, with their sometimes extremely painful lessons, are really challenges that can enable both partners in a relationship to reach their own heart and become more whole – as long as the phases are understood and used as such.

If, as partners, we are willing to tackle all the obstacles that are waiting for us in the course of a relationship, we will grow ever closer. All of a sudden there will be feelings that weren't there before. All of a sudden things will work out with an ease that was never there before. Sometimes we will be incredulous at all the new things we're finding in our old relationship. And at the same time, almost imperceptibly, a kind of peace is unfolding. And it doesn't feel stale or boring at all. In it, we can recuperate and revitalize each other. We feel safe and snug. There's no hint of restlessness, no desire for distraction and excitement. We experience how it feels to really share our life with someone else. This encourages our desire to open up even further.

There was a time when I discussed issues that were really important for me with my friends. We would be on the phone for hours and have conspiratorial meetings about our feelings that our husbands never ever had a clue about – and weren't meant to either. Today there is nobody who knows me better and knows more about my feelings than my husband, even though he sees the world fundamentally differently from me. No one is closer to me than he is. That doesn't mean that we don't argue or have misunderstandings. But we use conflicts more and more readily as signposts for the next step in our marriage. After everything we have experienced and resolved so far, the disagreements don't push us into questioning the marriage itself any more.

When real partnership is unfolding in a relationship, sometimes it seems to go back to the way it was at the beginning. Sometimes the feelings are even stronger than at the start. But this phase also has its challenges. Precisely because we are sharing so much with each other, our deepest pain finally shows up. Issues arise that up to now we have completely repressed. Power struggles flare up out of the blue and we can find them quite bizarre. Any rigidity in our partner feels very hurtful, and we run the risk of responding with impatience and incomprehension to seemingly long-resolved issues.

I well remember once, when my husband and I had already overcome a lot of difficulties, we were peacefully sitting in the car talking about something trivial. Then within ten minutes our harmless conversation had turned into a vicious argument. It was extraordinary. The battle lines were drawn in an instant, and we finished by concluding that it would *never* work between us. We'd had enough. That was it!

We sat there in shock, frozen into silence for a long while. However could we have got to this point again?! Well, we *had* got to this point again. But during this silence I realized 100 times faster than previously how insane all this was. My husband too seemed to make use of the frosty silence, because very subtly, without any words, the icy wasteland in our car began to thaw. It was fascinating. We were sitting next to each other saying nothing and the atmosphere between us was becoming palpably warmer – until at exactly the same moment we looked at each other and laughed.

As long as we are together, our mutual growth will challenge us and offer us more and more opportunities for profound healing, especially when something seems like a step backwards. Time and again our trust in the relationship will be challenged, and time and again we will be rewarded for every courageous step we take towards each other.

I am well aware that on this path of mutual growth it's not only both partners that can change but also the entire family and even life as a whole – sometimes dramatically. While I am writing this my husband is preparing dinner while larking about with four children in the kitchen. It might sound ridiculous, but for me this is a miracle. Only a few years ago it would have been completely impossible. Our roles in the marriage were clearly defined and we were trapped in them. Today we are both grateful – my husband for the fact that he no longer feels a guest in his own house, has finally integrated into the family and now recognizes that his creativity can revive his home life, and me because I finally have the space to go out without leaving a vacuum behind. I am only able to write this book straight from the heart because my husband is willing to serve us all straight from the heart.

The word 'serve' might sound like a dusty old relic from a bygone era. Some people might associate it with self-denial or self-sacrifice. I believe that service is one of the most fundamental characteristics of a powerful and growing relationship. If you serve another person from the heart, you experience that you have something to give, and that brings you strength and power.

5

Lust or no lust – that is the question...

When it comes to sex, English-speaking people often describe it as 'making love', whereas in other languages it is more about 'having sex'. For me, it's neither 'having sex' nor 'making love'. I prefer to regard it as 'letting love flow', and as such consider it one of the best-kept secrets in the Western world.

Hardly anything we know about this fulfilling flow between two bodies is communicated to us in a natural way, even though in this day and age we are being constantly flooded with sexual stimulation and naked images. No other area between men and women is filled with so much promise, so much confusion and so much hurt. These days it seems that almost anything goes. However, this does not provide the wonderful passion and satisfaction we might have expected, but guilt and harrowing self-doubt. Our natural sexuality has been subsumed by a rather technical approach. We have often lost contact with our real passion and have no idea how easily we can express ourselves sexually, how powerfully our feelings can flow and how they can fill us and our partners with love. Sex has been robbed of its natural innocence and it has been replaced by the expectation that everything is possible. And so people get lost more and more often and don't know where they are any more.

Today we face a constant barrage of sexual information. Quite 'normal' women's magazines feature articles with the headlines: 'Blow-jobs – How to give them properly', 'Lust through pain' or 'What men need'. With regard to sex, competition in the media is fierce and so we are constantly challenged to achieve more and more in our sex lives. Magazines promise more fulfilment by relentless comparisons: 'Test your sexual positions – which ones are best for you and your partner?' and 'How often do you do it? More than once a week?'

It is not surprising when adults run out of steam under this all-pervasive pressure. Even more serious is its effect on young people. One teen-magazine article described a young girl who was terribly disappointed by her first kiss. After studying an article on 25 different ways of kissing, she had come to the frustrated conclusion: 'I tried to do it exactly like that, but it didn't feel right.'

Nowadays young people can scrutinize how others have sex. They can 'consume' sex by watching 'dirty clips' on the music channels or in the romantic settings of early evening soaps where only the most beautiful, sensitive and irresistible people do it. All teenage magazines offer endless sexual advice and technical tips. Adolescents who are preoccupied with exploring their own identity and are full of doubts about their body and attractiveness are being flooded with images of perfect multiple orgasms on every channel.

But all this doesn't seem to function as a guideline for young viewers. A poll among 14 to 17 year olds revealed that only one third of this age group had had sexual intercourse and that the first time for nearly half the girls had been either 'nothing special', 'unpleasant' or guilt-ridden. Research done by the German Ministry of Health concluded that the pressure of sexual imagery on inexperienced teenagers was so great that most girls doing it for the first time worried primarily about 'doing it right'. According to another poll, one third of all youngsters was already worried about not being good enough in bed.

To have sex or to make love?

Speaking as an experienced therapist, I believe that hardly anybody is aware how much emotional and physical damage this sexual fast-food is causing. Time and again I meet people who are ashamed because they haven't had sex for years or have never found any real fulfilment in it. Poll results telling them bluntly that everybody else is having more fun than them only confirm their feelings of failure. According to the polls, German couples do it at least twice a week, East Berliners twice a night and one third of the people we see in the supermarket, at the gym or in the street enhance their numerous sexual encounters with whipped cream, champagne or leather outfits.

Those statistics claim that everything is possible for *other people*. They completely confuse people about their real physical needs, their sexual fragility and their sense of modesty. In reality, there is hardly any difference between normal statistics and statistics about people's sex lives. Even in polls by renowned and serious institutes guaranteeing complete anonymity, nearly one third of anxious and inhibited people never give any answers at all. Questions regarding the frequency of sex, preferred practices and kinds of stimulants definitely remain unanswered. And as for the rest? Who would confess to feeling like a failure?

Researchers for an American poll tried new methods to get closer to the truth. They questioned nearly 3,000 people and repeated the questions up to 15 times. The results: one quarter of the men and nearly one third of the women admitted to not having had sex at all during the past year. Another quarter had only had it a few times.

TV, advertising, the internet and a whole variety of magazines suggest more or less directly that sensuality, eroticism and passion are normal and available for everyone. So if our intimate life has nothing of this glamour, this vitality and inner fulfilment, then we start pretending, both to ourselves and others. We abandon ourselves to images in our head rather than to our real partner, we dress up or we simply feel wrong and inadequate. A client once started a session with 'I feel like a leper' and confessed, in tears, that for a long time she had not wanted sex. In bed with her husband she had either faked an orgasm or stimulated herself with exciting thoughts and images. Afterwards she would often disappear to the bathroom to cry and wash herself. I've heard stories like that from many women.

Men, meanwhile, often feel swamped by shame and self-contempt when confessing to an almost addictive consumption of pornography or regular visits to prostitutes. A while ago I was waiting for someone in my car, parked in the city centre around midday in front of a pornographic cinema and peep show. While I was waiting there, one man after the other came out of the door. I wondered what it would be like to be all alone in a cubicle or a seat in a cinema with just a couple of tissues. From what I had heard in therapy I could tell what those men just had experienced, what they had got rid of and what they had gained. I looked into their faces. They were men of all ages and nationalities – men in sharp suits, men in grubby tracksuit bottoms with greasy hair, small men, tall men, fat men, skinny men... As different as they seemed, they had one thing in common – their eyes were dead and they all came out looking shifty. They seemed restless, as if haunted by other people's eyes or their own shame. Watching them walk away, I felt great sadness and compassion. How they must all have yearned to actually make a woman happy!

Men often tell me why they buy sex or images of sex, why they secretly spend a small fortune in brothels or spend whole nights looking at porn on the net after their wives have gone to bed. What they describe sounds like a disease, an addiction, and it nearly always has its roots in their presumed inadequacy. In the darkest recesses of their mind they are saying, 'I am a failure. I couldn't make my wife happy any more, couldn't reach her, make her open up to me...' And somewhere in their body there is a passionate desire to free themselves, to let themselves go and to really connect with someone.

Perfect images, perfect partners, perfect positions...

Whether it stems from Hollywood movies, statistics or adverts, men as well as women are submitting more and more to the pressure of this ubiquitous chase for perfect images, perfect partners, perfect positions and a perfect performance. Eventually they are driven by the desire to do *everything* perfectly.

In my view it is this pressure to achieve and the resulting emotional and mental exhaustion that primarily prevent physical love these days. Everyone is obsessed with the frequency of lovemaking. You simply *have* to do it twice a week, and if it's only twice a month that's serious evidence of sexual inadequacy. But these demands, this measuring up and comparing, simply lay the foundations for the disappearance of lust. Nothing is more important for physical love than relaxation and leisure. Instead it is viewed in a technical and controlled way, and, weighed down by fantasies and utopias, loses all perspective. At the beginning of this book I claimed that 70 per cent of all divorces were unnecessary. I have also come to the conclusion, judging by number of shameful faces distorted by addiction that I see, that in an equally high number of marriages there has been either no sex for years or the sex has become a matter of routine without any romance at all.

Nobody dares to admit that they don't have sex very much. Even those who courageously ignore society's demands for a certain quantity find it difficult to express that though they comply to statistical normality they lack a certain something, that somewhere inside they are haunted by emptiness. Countless long-term couples feel trapped in a repetitious cycle of sex. There is hardly ever anything new or creative about it, let alone any magic. Sexy lingerie, porn videos, role-playing, swinger clubs, changing partners – none of it gives them the scope for a real mind and body encounter. There may still be love between the partners, but they are unable to genuinely express it in a physical way. This invariably leads to a slow withering away of the relationship or to an increasing number of arguments. Sooner or later separation seems to be the only way out.

In my mind, if sex becomes a dead-end street, it can blow apart any relationship. But separation, particularly if it's rooted in the bedroom, doesn't solve the real problem. Sooner or later the old restlessness is back and the search goes on for the chance to connect sex and soul and express love in a physical way. It is a search driven by a deep human desire – a desire that permeates every corner of our lives, that overcomes all conventions and morals, that in the long run is stronger than all the euphoria at the beginning of a new relationship and that cannot be fulfilled by pornography and sexual fantasy. It is a desire that reminds us of our real challenge: to give ourselves to another person, just as we are, and to love them back in the same way.

The sexual dead-end street

And so we stumble on, keeping a count of how often we make love, checking on our practices and our partners. Hardly anybody experiences the real, deep, nurturing power of physical love or realizes its powerful spiritual dimension. In terms of sexuality, nearly everybody would be best off starting again from scratch. It would be liberating if we could confess to each other that we don't know anything or that nothing we do know leads us to what we desire. If we dared to do this, we could meet our partner again in all innocence and truthfulness, and we could open up physically and heal. But we don't hear anything about this process in the media or in society as a whole, and we don't learn about it in our educational system either.

There is a huge lack of knowledge about physical love. To talk about the natural flow of love in our Western society is like talking of snow in a desert. Young people have technically-orientated sex education and are then left to struggle on alone in their search for intimacy. These days we have easier, earlier and more frequent sexual experiences than ever before, but they lead to easier, earlier and more frequent insecurity, anxiety and shame. Instead of experiencing sexuality as a natural life-force, many young people doubt themselves and distrust their own body. Sex remains unprocessed, an inner shadow in the body, only to be activated later in life with every attempt to make physical love. Most of the time we have no idea why we then feel cold, frigid or impotent, or are always craving new affairs.

We want everything but feel nothing

Our love life is polarized, with a wide gap between 'want it all the time' and 'don't feel like doing it at all'. And it might come as a surprise to you, but they are equally unsatisfying.

If we don't feel lust at all, we feel numb and dead. Often our heart has been broken. Somewhere along the way our dream of true love and satisfying sex has been destroyed by possessiveness, jealousy, sacrifice, greed, distrust and betrayal. Bit by bit we have withdrawn from our bodily sensations and cut ourselves off from our sexuality. We may even condemn it. But even when we repress our pain and deny our deep-seated desire for physical love, sex still retains its power over us, only in the form of its shadow.

One of our favourite shadows is our partner. If we repress our desires, for our partner everything is about sex. They always want it, dream of it. They can always do it. And if we don't let them, they simply go out – to parties, bars, websites, peep shows or prostitutes.

If, on the other hand, we control our sexuality without immediately encountering a sensual or lustful shadow either inside or outside us, something in our life hardens. Something dies. We become a 'better' person, but dead.

Either way, the sexual impulse remains powerful. If we don't heal our wounds, if we repress our pain and control it, then it turns into a kind of guerrilla fighter threatening our life from all quarters. In the end we can flee into being dull, self-righteous or judgemental, or attend to our wounds and reconnect to our heart and sexuality. Then the sexual flow returns to us more or less naturally.

It's not only those who deny or repress their desires who have problems. Insatiable lovers also suffer from heartache. Changing sexual partners frequently often reveals a desperate search for love. All those Casanovas storming one bedroom after the other and all those ever-willing seductresses are not sex gods and goddesses at all – they are lost, searching with the body for what can only be found with the heart. Their hearts have been broken, just like those of the people who are eternally numb, and they don't want to feel the pain any more either. But they haven't given up – they are fighting, searching and challenging. They are driven on by the lure of a new thrill, a new conquest.

Whenever we treat sex like a drug we really are busy healing old wounds. We are looking for a connection we didn't make before. We might have wanted to give love and only got sex back. We might have wanted to give our heart and been trapped by possessiveness. It might be all in the past, but it's still there inside us, so we are constantly looking for connections and never finding them, and if we do find them, we can't stay and make something of them, as we still have this old divide between our body and our heart.

Nowadays there is hardly a person or a relationship that doesn't need sexual healing. When couples come to me in crisis, they usually describe one of two kinds of sex. 'We haven't had sex for quite a while' is one statement. The other one is: 'Nothing works any more, whereas before it was always fine in bed.' In the first case it's obvious that the connection between the two partners has been severed. The same is also true for the second, as I know from experience. And affairs and all kinds of pornographic addictions are found in sexually barren relationships as well as in sexually active ones.

Sex as a weapon

When Rebecca came to me she was in shock. She had found out that her husband had been visiting brothels regularly for some time. 'But it was always so good in bed,' she said, shaking her head. Why did her husband visit prostitutes? She couldn't understand it at all.

In the course of our sessions it turned out that sex had long been the most powerful weapon in the power struggle that was their marriage. Rebecca had played with her body and with her husband. Sometimes, when she couldn't reach him in any other way, she had seduced him. She often did what he wanted, but only to dominate him later. Sometimes he was 'allowed' to have her because she wanted more time with him. Sometimes she rejected him in order to feel her own power over him. At parties they very quickly went their own ways and flirted with other people in front of each other – but only up to a certain point.

In one session, when Rebecca was very graphically describing sex with her husband, she said how something had 'clicked' with her: 'I was pressed up against the headboard because he was pushing so hard. And that pain triggered something in me. It abruptly pulled me out of my fantasy world and I realized that my body didn't want all this. For a moment I felt like crying. But the feeling vanished very quickly and I carried on furiously.'

Rebecca discovered that there was hardly any real intimacy in her marriage, that she rarely confided her desires to her husband and that their lives were very busy – as busy as they were in bed. She also found that they rarely experienced any real togetherness and connection. Most of all she realized that she had always, from day one, been afraid of losing her husband. When they had met he had been in another relationship and it had been a while before he had chosen Rebecca. Ever since then she'd been plagued by insecurity. She had never had the feeling that he had committed himself whole-heartedly to her. So whenever she was afraid that he might leave her or cheat on her she got a kick out of seducing him. She always felt she had to prove herself – and that roused her passion. But her heart had never been at rest in the relationship. She had never felt really loved.

At a later stage Rebecca's husband came to the sessions as well. He hadn't fared any better. 'My wife is always making demands on me,' he mused. 'I'm never good enough. She's always nagging me. Our marriage has been very demanding.' They had indeed had sex ever more frequently and intensely, but he had felt emptier and emptier.

When sex is used as a weapon it becomes empty, greedy or lifeless. Sometimes it is used to manipulate those we claim to love. Often it determines levels of dependency, worthlessness and attractiveness in a relationship. We use our bodies to attract others or to keep them away. And all that detracts from our own physical power and robs sex of its healing effect.

There's one feeling most frequently linked to sex: fear. But sex is the medium of love, a gateway to giving, a way of making meaningful contact with another person and putting aside our loneliness. Look at how babies are naturally connected to their own vitality. Sex is our most natural way of communication. It should be fun. It can build bridges and can express the love that we feel.

The second part of this book will examine lust and love in more detail. For now, let's turn our attention to men and women.

6

'Battle-axes' and 'wimps'

We all yearn for harmony and unity between the sexes – only to find out in the end that men do indeed come from Mars and women from Venus. However, the fact that the two sexes function in different ways isn't really bad news for a relationship. Quite the reverse: a really successful emotional partnership needs the different kinds of male and female strength. The real problem lies elsewhere. Too many representatives of the fairer sex have mutated into battle-axes and too many masters of creation have degenerated into wimps. Women have lost their natural femininity and men their natural masculinity.

It takes some courage and patience to get to the heart of your relationship problems, but you will find that these days – at the beginning of the twenty-first century – there is a lot of hatred of men and fear of women. Both are hardened and distorted forms of what were originally truly divine elemental powers.

A woman is receptive by nature. She is physically predetermined to receive a man inside her, to open up for him. A man is built to be giving. He is able to move, to enliven, to fertilize. In therapy I often use an image that sums it all up for me: a woman is like a lake, a man like a river flowing into the lake. The health, vitality and clarity of the lake are mainly dependent on the quality of the river that feeds it. If the river is polluted, if poison or sewage is constantly pumped into it on its way to the lake, this will inevitably reach the lake too. Every lake is only as good as the river that feeds it.

I am aware that at this time of emancipation and equal rights this image might appear old-fashioned or even reactionary, and might trigger vehement protest. But it symbolizes the truth. If you accept it just for a moment and take on board its true meaning you will discover the groundbreaking force that can be unleashed when men and women return to their true being.

When women constantly try to change their men, nag them and want to be as powerful as them, then they are trying to protect themselves from further hurt or, to stay with the metaphor, to protect their lake from further pollution from the river. Such behaviour is like damming the river, but as a result the lake slowly dries out.

When women start to remodel their men, when they argue and nag, when they begin to rule from behind the scenes and act with an active male power, they lose their receptivity, their devotion and their softness. They harden up and turn into imitations of men. And that's exactly why – consciously or not – they denounce men. 'Oh, *men...*' is a phrase that can be heard all over the place nowadays. It's said in a seemingly maternal but smirking way, but in reality it is quite bitter. It expresses a silent undercurrent of contempt.

In former times women either put up with their lot or manipulated men by withdrawing their love. Today they either compete with men, indulge in vague fantasies or, full of bitterness, petition for divorce. Instead they should believe in the infinitely transformative power of their love and the seismographic accuracy of their intuition. How often I have met women who knew very early on that something in their life or their relationship was wrong. But only very few trusted their instincts and gathered together enough courage to follow their intuition.

How often do female bodies respond to male behaviour with a disorder, how often does a female mind react to male strategies and systems with anxiety – and how rarely do women really trust their bodies and their minds and act accordingly? How often do women really believe in the transforming power of their own love? How often do women trust in the validity of their feelings? How often do women follow their heart? How often do women fight side by side with their men, with all their female devotion, all their love, all their faith and all consequences, for a new path, a new way forward in their relationship? Too often they withdraw in the face of the competent and dominant behaviour of their men – in the face of their practical knowledge, their facts and figures, their rationalizations, their financial power. Women keep silent, they manipulate or seduce, but they never stand by their intuition and never consider their faith and their love to be the real source of their power. Many women moan about an economic and political system shaped by male ambition and a demand for continuous growth, and about relationships dominated by male ignorance. But what do they do? They don't trust the infinite power of their own love which they could use to create different systems and new kinds of relationships.

Women's liberation has not allowed women to really come into their own. It has given them new freedoms and opened up new areas for them. Women have been able to be independent, responsible, creative and ingenious, but too many women, in the struggle with a male-dominated system, have become entangled in that very system. Women have decried the sad mess male supremacy has made of their lives, but they have called for defiance, not for femininity. Most of all, they have not looked at their own contribution to the problem, their own willingness to sacrifice themselves and their own lack of faith in their abilities. In their battle to emerge from the shadow of male supremacy, they have frequently not drawn strength from their unique female power but have become even more hard, bitter and ruthless than the men.

In spite of this, lots of things have changed for women. At least in our culture they aren't suppressed any more, they don't have to take second place. Women know their rights and the possibilities open to them and they can make their own decisions. The vast majority of divorces, for example, are initiated by women. But deep inside our female psyche there is a dark recess filled with fear of male dominance, of male sexuality, a fear which automatically feeds into an equally hidden corner of our minds – the one filled with hatred of men.

The wails of wounded women

I once went to a workshop for couples. On one of the days the sexes were separated. The women went off on their own to deal exclusively with their female roots. The same applied to the men. Hardly anything in my life has surprised and moved me as much as what I experienced that day. At one point, every one of the maybe 20 women in the room was given a small mirror and asked to find a quiet space in the room. The task was to undress and for about half an hour to contemplate their breasts and their genitalia. The women were supposed to enter into an inner dialogue with their body, to listen to it, to feel with it, to remember everything that their breasts and genitalia had experienced in their lives and the memories they had stored. After about ten minutes quiet sobbing could be heard here and there in the otherwise silent room. After a while it developed into a fearsome crying and howling that encompassed the whole group, became louder and louder and eventually filled the room with a veritable lament.

Eventually the women were asked to get dressed again and to regroup. Then they were asked to give their bodies the opportunity to express all the strength and energy hidden underneath this sadness. Wild earthy music was played. The women were asked to move to its rhythm and express whatever sounds they spontaneously came up with. Again there were a few minutes of tension and anxiety, but then everyone – mothers, students, businesswomen – turned into wild furies, wrathful warriors, angry Amazons. The room seemed to explode with the sound of their stomping feet and their threatening, accusing and powerful shrieks. What I experienced that day went far beyond shared personal suffering – it was a kind of arch-experience of being a woman.

We don't just have an individual unconscious, we also share a collective unconscious – our social and historical heritage. If the genetic material of a female cell could tell us about its last few centuries, it would talk of submission, rape, slavery, witch-hunts and numerous children born either alive or dead. Even in the twentieth century, it would probably only have known for a few decades that it could experience an orgasm. The same cell would carry information about illegal, secret and life-threatening abortions. It would know about marital duties, financial dependency and unwanted pregnancies. A cell of the recent past would tell of battles for recognition, workplace ambitions and physical freedom. But this would be only a fraction of its genetic material.

Tomorrow's female cell would know that its predecessors had only achieved half of their stored potential. It would know that it only had brought to life a tiny fraction of its infinite female power. It would know that the reservoir of love dormant in it would be enough to transform the world. It would know that the body of the woman to which it belonged was a precise seismographic instrument that she could trust completely. True emancipation would mean being rooted in self-responsibility and freedom while being at the same time deeply, naturally and firmly connected with life. True competence would mean being instinctively connected with all knowledge regarding life and the planet. The cell would know that the woman to which it belonged would not have to liberate herself from anything but could commit fully to her own boundless source, her heart.

In a real sense, the true nature of womanhood is not about having children and a career. It is about a natural, instinctive, healthy way of dealing with children, jobs and life as a whole. It is about an intangible universal connection and a deep heartfelt power intrinsically linked to life itself. It is about an all-embracing acceptance of life, far beyond any self-sacrifice. It is about the kind of knowledge that simply exists and cannot be learned.

If a relationship seems to be either about the man or the woman, it is really about either the head or the heart. When I mentioned this connection to a man who had recently been deserted by his wife, he explained, 'In the end I had to recognize that my head was nothing more than a kind of airbag. My head seems to run after truths that were proven a long time ago. It analyzes, ponders, researches, searches and eventually discovers that the Earth isn't flat – it's round. But the Earth has always been round and always will be. That's the point!'

I think what applies to our planet applies to the true nature of women as well. The Earth has always been round and never thinks twice about it. It is round and it can't be anything else – even if the whole male world still believes that it is flat. It is round and it is alive. And it has no other choice than to be just that and to wait for the recognition of this truth by the men who live on it.

There is an instinctive power in women that many of them have either buried or don't take seriously any more – a power that simply *knows*. It is all-embracing and connected to everything. A woman who reconnects to it, who starts to live accordingly and learns to trust herself again doesn't capitulate. Instead she organizes her life according to natural laws. Such a woman knows when she feels fulfilled, when she is loved and whom she can love. She won't live according to any external expectations, won't bow down to men and won't sacrifice herself to her children. She will expect to be respected and loved as a matter of course. At best she will be a great mystery to men; at worst she will follow a simplistic female logic that will drive the male mind crazy and make so-called logical conversations impossible. A wise man once said: 'You men have to understand that you have to love women, not understand them. *That* is what has to be understood.'

Dreaming of knights in shining armour

In the very beginning, in early societies, male supremacy was based on physical superiority. Since then, other values, valid for both sexes, have gained in importance. But even though we left those early ways behind a long time ago, they are still anchored firmly at the back of our minds. Just as experiences and influences from childhood shape the way we respond as adults, as a species we have retained attitudes and behaviour from the past that are counterproductive in the world today.

Both men and women know now that men are not supreme and that physical power is not the most important quality in a person. In fact we have known this for some time. So why, in spite of this knowledge, did women remain disadvantaged for so long? How could they be denied their birthright of equality until not so very long ago? How could their natural way of expressing their emotional, mental and spiritual equality with men have been suppressed for such a long time? It would be all too easy to claim that women were victims of men and their traditional claims of superiority. What have women contributed to this battle of the sexes?

In the same way that to this day women's cells contain memories of the dark days of rape and submission, in spite of all our conscious demands for equality and freedom, we still have secret longings for a strong man and a noble saviour. Our history does not only contain oppression. It also contains the fact that for a long time we chose the easy way out in order to be protected and provided for. To this day women abdicate their responsibilities and leave it to men to make decisions, to provide for them and to battle through the trials and tribulations of life. Many women initially enjoy being kept from the battlefields of the workplace and being provided for by their men. To begin with they may also admire the men for their capabilities and for the status and lifestyle they are able to give them.

Not many women would admit it, but often women don't marry a man for himself but for his potential – the promising student, the able craftsman, the successful manager, the talented artist, the wealthy businessman, the noble heir. Once, in the course of the marriage, this potential has turned into success, wealth and security, the women are often bewildered. They have what they wanted – but they don't feel what they expected to feel.

This kind of success doesn't bring real life into a family. It initially drains the men and eventually – and inevitably – the partnership too. During the relationship the women are forced to discover how deficient the male way of life is. They learn that it leads to wealth and social status, but at the same time it is a dead-end street and doesn't provide long-lasting satisfaction for them. In the end, dependent on their men and their deficiencies, the women punish them with their contempt. Nevertheless they stay in their marriage, full of inner resentment and afraid of losing the superficial comforts of their dependency.

Women are often dissatisfied with their men's work and disappointed by their own lives, and deep down in their memories are so shaped by their own idea of worthlessness that they still refuse to trust their own power and strength and eventually take responsibility for their own lives. And so the responsibility remains with the men, and with it all the blame for the state of the planet, the economy, politics, families, sex – and women.

'See what it's like for us!' 'See how empty our lives are!' 'Look how much we've sacrificed for our families!' 'We're exhausted!' women complain, with all the self-importance of martyrdom. Many are convinced that their children won't make it in the world unless they support them. Many feel obliged to save them from the irresponsible attitude of their divorced husbands. Many believe that in order to create a balance of love in this world they have to sacrifice their own life to their man's career. A feminist once summarized those female laments sarcastically as: 'The only payback that life is offering us women is the fact that men die earlier.'

Of course, apart from the complaining sisterhood whose lives are nothing more than being a taxi for the children, doing housework and performing socially acknowledged part-time jobs, there are the so-called 'better men' – women who are like men, only better. A friend of mine who works for an international fashion house recently declared: 'Even in the world of fashion, women in positions of power are becoming more and more asexual. They are smart and elegant, but without any feminine expression or preferences.' If you want to have a career as a woman, apparently you have to learn to 'play the game' and 'adapt'.

The complaining sisters and the 'better men' are only two extremes of the female confusion and the general confusion in our society. Between those two poles there are countless variations on the female search for fulfilment and self-realization. The women's movement of recent decades holds many truths, but in the end they are only half-truths. The point is not to fight your way to the top or to resign when faced with male supremacy. It is to finally recognize your own freedom and strength as a woman.

The complete truth is that women indeed boast the same intelligence and creativity and the same psychological strength as men. But for them to really reap the benefits of women's liberation and take their true place in society, they have to admit to their own part in the discrimination. The more unhappy women are about the male success which determines their lives, the more powerless they feel, the more resentful, the more they blame, nag and scold, the more they rebel, the stronger their secret and mostly unconscious desire to abdicate responsibility for their own lives, to play the victim and to rely on men to provide for them.

Behind every discontented woman there is a weak man

Of course these discontented, rebellious and self-sacrificing women have men – frequently the kind that shy away from their own power. For quite a while now men have been involved in an exhausting competition with their peers. Testing their strength, winning or surrendering is written into every one of their cells. The dismal cycle men have been trapped in for thousands of years is one of power struggles, defeats and compensation. Winning used to be an indispensable part of being a man and in the pursuit of victory men always had to reckon that one day they might be defeated by someone stronger. But at no time would a man be allowed to show that fear. He always had to convince himself and others of his power and strength, even when he had none. Or he had to find weaker men in order to feel strong again.

These days being a man still means using up a lot of energy in hiding weakness and compensating for it. Only very few men train their bodies to be strong. These days the male species relies on the fuel-injection engine rather than muscle power. And in many cases, the challenges of life are met analytically and intellectually – the game happens in the mind alone.

Most men know their strengths and abilities and understand practical matters, but they don't know what they need to find peace and happiness. They know how the world works, but they don't feel its vitality. And they hardly ever have a clue what is happening in their soul. They often deny its existence altogether, so that they don't have to deal with it at all. Most men know about *things* and can analyze how they fit together, but they don't experience love – they confuse it with the excitement of conquest and have no idea of the mystery of the heart. They don't even know that their head will never understand their heart.

On the other hand, there are many things women don't understand – they simply *know* them. This kind of knowledge doesn't require a process of analysis – it simply exists and becomes real if it is attended to. The heart has no arguments ready to explain this kind of knowledge; it cannot give reasons for it or scientifically prove it. Because of this, the heart's knowledge is rarely recognized or taken seriously in our society. If you follow your heart you are extremely vulnerable, because you can never say 'because', 'therefore' or *quod erat demonstrandum*. The head is given more respect. The head is logical and rational. It can deduct, substantiate and prove. It can explain every object – but it cannot experience it. It chases after the truth without ever accessing its inner power.

Only men who have made contact with their natural connection with life can really have an effect on the world, the economy, and their families and their women. When a man follows his real strength, he can invigorate and stimulate. He can be fruitful. Most of all, such a man is sure of himself and his capacity for love – which is the foundation for being able to give love so that the wife by his side doesn't slowly shrivel up.

But nearly everything men do is unconsciously about hiding their vulnerable side and ensuring that their external power is recognized. A man leaves the house in the morning claiming he is going out to provide for his family. In the evening he exercises, allegedly to get fitter. He loves fast cars because speed is fun. But really he is competing with other men and looking for victory and power in everything he does. All that serves to confirm his real value to him, because he has no idea what it is otherwise. All that is supposed to give his life something that he has forgotten – meaning. It gives meaning to all those things that he has created, improved, fought for and destroyed. Again and again.

When this man comes home at night, he seldom asks himself: 'What was the point of all those things I did today? What difference did they make? Who is better off because I exist?' He might well have done a great deal that could really nurture his wife and his family. But he only knows the results of his actions. He doesn't know himself.

Many very successful men experience a simple cold as a life-threatening disease. Countless men stare helplessly at flower shops, their children playing and the smooth texture of their wives' skin. So many men are creative, strategically experienced conquerors but deflate in the face of everyday emotional life like pricked balloons. On a deeper level, with their long history of chasing success and victory, they have learned to cut off their uncomfortable feelings and to fake their strength. That is why they turn to intellect and power in situations where intuition and a connection with life are called for. Cut off from their feelings, they fear the flood of female emotion. They are completely unprepared for it. Far away from their emotional homeland, they are dependent on feminine intuition and the wealth of women's feelings.

Female breadwinners, male housewives

So men are just as chained to the game of head against heart, power against powerlessness, as women are. And as neither of the sexes is connected to its real power, each demands it from the other. Women look for protection and care, but are full of resentment when they have to pay for it with their autonomy. Men insist on freedom and power, but are forced to live on second-hand feelings and to look after an allegedly inferior person. Both are tired of this either/or game. And it has not served either. Women have become hardened in their fight for equality and turned into battle-axes; men, behind their masks of independence, have become more and more helpless and degenerated into wimps. Both feel betrayed by this polarization.

A healthy individual has feminine as well as masculine strengths – strengths that are simply expressed in different ways and ideally complement each other. When men and women want to contribute their respective qualities to their relationship, each partner needs a minimum in autonomy and responsibility. Thanks to women's lib we know now that women have just as much potential as men. But do we dare to claim that they need just as much autonomy, responsibility and financial freedom as men do? Women of all ages have shown me that a woman who really wants to give herself has to feel free and able to make decisions for herself. To do that, she has to learn to shoulder the responsibility for her own life. The truth is that if a relationship is to last, women have to stand on their own two feet more and more – materially, intellectually and emotionally.

I don't think that being a woman means being a selfless housewife and mother. Being a woman means being free, instinctive and receptive in your heart. It means actively demonstrating to your husband and children how potent and rich life is when you are led by the heart. And being a man doesn't mean being the best, but being yourself – with confidence. Being a man doesn't mean withdrawing from feelings, instincts, wife and family in order to bear the responsibility for everything.

I think a truly healthy relationship develops when both men and women realize their potential, when both work and earn money and both look after their children and take care of their own personal development. I believe that husbands who are sole providers and rare visitors to the family home can never regain their emotional integrity – and their heart. And I believe that women who sacrifice themselves, who are 'always there for everybody' but who nurture nothing but the household and the family, can never unleash their full female power and never give themselves wholly.

Leaders of the hearts of men

A man once explained to me, 'Women who really love don't make any demands. They don't want men to provide for them, they don't want them to protect them, they just want them to love them.' I have learned that women need this kind of love in order to focus completely on their inner perception, to find their inner calm and to feel fulfilled in themselves. That way they can find, and feel, their own love inside. Only then can they realize their full potential and access their natural wisdom.

A man who experiences what happens to a woman who truly feels sustained in that way, even if it's only once, and a woman who feels truly recognized and fulfilled by a man can't pretend any more. They become courageous and play for high stakes – sometimes for a career, social recognition and a social network all in one. Men and women who truly comple-ment and understand each other can change the world.

For me, this return to a real femininity and masculinity is the real adventure of life. The more deeply we get to know each other, the fewer real differences we will discover, and more natural attraction and complementary qualities will emerge from under the mountain of contemporary confusion and the millennia of conditioning. In my experience, women are the pioneers on this path to greater intimacy. Men and women alike only reach their destination when women, in the true sense of the word, trust their own instinctive leadership more than male resistance and factual dominance.

It is women who have to lead the way through the thicket back to the heart. It's no use whingeing any longer that men deny this and repress that, that they are emotional robots and psychological idiots. Women should dry their tears, take themselves seriously at last, stride forth with courage and make something better and more meaningful of their lives. This will both strengthen them personally and enhance their careers and give them more meaning. It will change their relationships and have more of an impact on their men than a thousand nagging words. And it will heal their children.

Anna was a single woman, the only woman in an all-male office. When she came to me, it was not the first time she had had therapy. By now she had acquired a fair bit of psychological knowledge and could describe and analyze each of her symptoms in detail.

A short while ago her GP had given her a sick note because of her mental state and had recommended that she attend a day clinic. She explained that she had been crying for two weeks and would certainly break down during the session if she told me what was happening to her. She began to describe what she felt and thought – about men, life in general, her fears and inadequacies and her role in her family of origin as the strange one, the mad one, the mentally fragile one. After every second sentence, she stopped and hesitantly checked with me whether what she was saying sounded crazy. I told her time and again that I rarely consider a way of seeing the world as crazy, and certainly not hers.

Anna didn't sob her way through her sessions. One morning she was very perky and actually began to laugh, even though she was telling me about all sorts of fears and anxieties. Eventually she declared that she hadn't felt so normal for a long time. 'I don't think I am mad at all,' she said. 'I simply need the courage to say what I think. Particularly to my family...'

A few days later I heard that Anna had been committed to a clinic at the urgent request of her family. Immediately after our session she had gone to see them and declared that there might be a good reason for her endless tears and that her mental state might not be so bad after all. As a result her family had declared her completely mad.

I don't know what happened to Anna, but I know that she was not mad when she came to see me. She was simply one of the many women who don't trust intuition and their feelings. In rational conversations she often had nothing to say and she felt alien amongst her male colleagues. She also had physical desires for tenderness and love that had little to do with her real sexual experiences. Over the years she had tried to hide her feelings more and more and as a result had been overwhelmed by them more and more often.

Anna never thought that her strange feelings might be giving her the right signals. She never thought that her body and her soul were in fact asking for the right stuff. She lacked the courage to say 'no' or to stand up for her feelings. All this had led to her slowly withdrawing from life, not feeling attractive any more and distrusting her femininity. By the time she saw me, she was too shy to date men and afraid of further sexual encounters. But behind all this she had a deep desire for a meaningful and fulfilling relationship with a man.

Ultimately, women have no other choice but to trust themselves again. When they finally believe what their heart, instincts and bodies are saying, they can also begin to trust men and teach them how precious and important female power is. Without its warming, nourishing energy, life dies. Today our relationships, our economy, our religions, our planet and our men all lack the powerful and at the same time yielding female power. How often do women trust their feelings? How often do women follow their heart? How often do women fight for what they believe in?

7

Three's always a crowd

Relationship routines, the monotony of marriage, a silver wedding anniversary approaching... Everything is heavy, listless, tedious, lifeless. We know our partner's every move, know in advance how our conversations, fewer by the day, will go. We don't even raise issues any more, because we have heard the unsatisfactory answers all too often. We sense, and hear, criticism of ourselves and how we behave. We feel restricted and unnoticed. We have tried to get closer to our partner again and again and come up against an invisible wall. We have wanted to connect and instead been rebuffed by withdrawal and silence. Or rejected by judgements and demands.

Of course, we also share some good times, as a matter of routine. A lot functions automatically, and on important issues we can take our consensus for granted. And sometimes we are overcome by the memories of our first weeks together or we smile at an unexpected erotic touch. But then we become aware of the dull Here and Now again, and dream of exciting and unpredictable encounters. We feel like the German ex-minister who yearned for life. But as soon as we become aware of our dreams, we pull ourselves up sharply. We need to keep things going, so we push our dreams back down to the bottom of the iceberg and instead flick through the TV listings for a gripping programme.

And then, apparently quite out of the blue, a stranger comes into our life and we feel like new. All our boundaries seem to dissolve and we are ready for adventure. At last we can live and love again.

With a lover we frequently experience an intensity of emotion and an uninhibited sexuality that we have rarely known, and hardly ever during our marriage. We feel electric – alive and vibrant. Our body pulses with passion and a huge river of excitement and arousal takes us out of our mundane world. It is as if a swathe of sunlight has broken through the heavy fog of our normal family life.

We can't really make any decisions, can't plan, and definitely can't integrate anything of this into our everyday life. As if in a fever we wait for the next phone call, the next meeting, the next touch. The secret lover works like insulin for a diabetic. We need our regular dose, otherwise our vitality levels will drop. Without a regular supply, we are in danger of sinking back into the unbearable routine of everyday life. It would seem like a return to captivity, to that domestic prison in which we were always asking: 'Is this it?'

The secret lover as panacea

By having an affair, we have hope and purpose once more. We now have something that is much more exciting than the old familiar routine. We are living on a high of uncertainty, of novelty, of the forbidden. The risk gives us an adrenaline rush;

our heart races, its beat pounding through our whole body. Love is rationed, limited, forbidden and secret. Every word, every encounter, every touch is precious and rare, special, risky, illicit and dangerous. With every word, every meeting and every touch, we have to be as circumspect as a bank robber inching his way between sensors and alarm systems. We want to savour every precious moment of it and at the same time have to keep it secret. We can only experience limited relief with a good friend or a loyal confidante. Aside from that our happiness has to quietly implode. At all costs it must not be discharged into the outside world. Because out there are our partner, our children, our family – and most of all our guilt.

We have just been on cloud nine with our lover, and now, at the mere thought of our family, we are racked with guilt. Having just drunk deeply from the elixir of life, we find ourselves left with a poisoned chalice. We once had hopes for our marriage too, but what is left of them now? Home is a place of dutiful demands, safe habits, sad defeats and bitter resignation. We were fed up with a lot of it for quite a while, but now we can satisfy our hunger elsewhere, we feel like a traitor when we come home. We had promised to be responsible. Instead we have burdened ourselves with guilt and are now afraid of the consequences of our secret machinations. We had duties at home and had always meant to do the best for our partner. Instead, we have turned away from them and are living for our pleasure alone. Too often we were inhibited in our marriage or subjected to stale mechanical desires. Now we are enjoying ourselves elsewhere and feel free.

The following dynamics are normally unconscious, but happen nevertheless when we are cheating on our partner. In the outer world we give ourselves to our secret lover and experience our passion and vibrancy with them, while at the same time we feel guilty at home. Because our partner is there, embodying family, familiarity and closeness. Once a secret love enters our life, it automatically splits into two worlds that seem to be incompatible. We instinctively know that both have their place in our life, that somehow they belong together, but we don't have the faintest idea how they can be harmoniously combined. In love triangles there seems to be only black and white, either closeness and familiarity or vibrancy and passion. And once we have travelled between those two poles for a while, both become heavily laden with guilt. We don't do anybody justice – ourselves, our lover or our partner.

First the fun, then the guilt

It is in love triangles that we experience our deepest inner division. Such relationships always bring pain and heartbreak to everyone involved. In them, love is like an undercover rebel. All three parties are only united in one thing: they are all afraid of closeness – even though in the case of the secret lover it looks the complete opposite.

Some singles are forever drawn to people living in a stable relationship. The married lover seems to be perfect, ideal, a combination of everything that they've ever dreamed of – apart from the fact that they are tied to another person and somehow always a little out of reach. Because of that, great hopes are just as inevitable as great disappointments and they take turns in ever-shorter intervals.

Love triangles are *determined* by vague boundaries. There is a continual whirl of guessing, hoping, fearing and yearning, and nobody knows exactly where they are. When delving deeper into those dynamics, we find a certain inability to connect and fear of intimacy in everybody concerned.

The person in the middle feels as though they are straddling an abyss. They are mostly incapable of making decisions because each of their partners seems to embody half of what they desire. They move to and fro, checking out the advantages and disadvantages of being with one or the other and secretly dreaming of having both of them. If they do come to a decision, there is always the feeling of having lost something. But if they get stuck in the hide-and-seek between their partners, they feel trapped and slowly run dry.

The secret lover always partly desires the cosy and safe position held by the one being cheated on. Most of all, they are struggling with their distrust of that partner that is so desirable but so otherwise engaged. Can they really trust someone who is cheating on someone else? They are also struggling with the guilt of ruining a relationship. Even if the piggy in the middle were to choose them, how could they build a happy relationship out of the ruins of the one they had destroyed?

The role of the person being cheated on in this triangular dilemma is the most difficult one. Whatever is happening behind their back is mirroring something of their own emotional dynamics, however vehemently they might reject the idea. However inconceivable it may seem to them, they too feel like pulling out of the relationship. Often, by the time one partner leaves, it's been quite a while since the other was available. They weren't firmly anchored in the relationship and had never been able to commit from the heart.

I have often taken the cheated partner all the way back to the beginning of the relationship – and how often have we arrived at issues like 'I had never been with anybody else when I met my partner,' 'I wasn't sure whether I really wanted them,' 'I allowed myself to be swept off my feet,' 'I have sometimes asked myself whether they were really right for me,' 'I had had my doubts about the relationship for a while...' Even though it might look as though the deceived party has suffered the most heartbreak, the inner truth of the relationship is a different picture. How often have I asked someone who has just been left for someone else: 'And had you already begun to leave emotionally? Had you already started to doubt your partner, to withdraw your trust and your heart?' And in reply I've received a shamefaced nod.

The betrayed person always leaves first

When one partner leaves, it's because the other one has left a long time ago. This is a fact we often don't want to accept. We'd prefer a straightforward ruling: the one who cheats is bad and the one who was cheated on is good. But in my view the person who has been betrayed has often betrayed themselves. They may be someone who doesn't really stand up for themselves and their beliefs. Someone who has high expectations of the relationship. Someone who prefers not to get involved with the real, shop-soiled, less-than-perfect partner. Someone who has often been feeling dependent on their partner in one way or another but not dared to challenge that dependency, to appear vulnerable, to courageously follow their own truth and to trust their own strength.

And the one who does the cheating? Frequently people who take lovers say 'At last I felt accepted. At last I could simply let go. I didn't have to constantly match up to someone else's standards.' One man was surprised to admit, after a few of our sessions, 'In the beginning I thought I simply needed some good sex again. But then I realized that my heart was searching too. The relationship between my wife and me was never really warm. In the beginning maybe it was hot ... but it was never really nice and warm.'

We often end up in someone else's bed when our emotions have been dammed up for too long and we can't express an important aspect of ourselves. Then our life-force looks for an escape route. It drains away from our relationship and flows directly to where it can enter into a vibrant liaison – and so we hurtle into an affair.

Love triangles almost always develop when we emotionally withdraw from our partner and their explicit or implicit pressure, our own inhibitions, our feeling of inferiority and inner emotions; when we are not really ready and willing to commit ourselves and not prepared to do some work on our own healing. It is in such illicit relationships that we express our fear of real closeness. It is rare that the third party turns up randomly – usually it is at a time we are either frozen and silent with our partner or engaged in a constant power struggle.

While in our affair we experience ourselves as wild, lively, inspired and passionate, we are downhearted and disappointed at the same time. 'My partner really didn't have much going for them. I've missed out on so much for such a long time...' The last sentence is true. But the first isn't. The excitement wasn't lacking in our partner, but in our relationship – all that wildness, passion and inspiration. Yes, we *have* missed it! But because we have not allowed ourselves to feel it for a long time. We have played it safe, swallowed our words, numbed our feelings, repressed our emotions, given up, lost heart and let our relationship drift into a routine. Now here comes a stranger and we believe that they have brought all those wonderful things with them and that they are responsible for them. In reality we have simply become involved again, become spontaneous again, been able to take a risk. And that is why we experience something with a stranger that we have not dared to give to our marriage.

When the third party turns up, it is high time ... not to make a decision between them but to face up to the truth. Go to your partner, sit down with them and explain yourself. Imagine a text template with some empty brackets:

> *Whenever you are thinking of [your lover], be grateful for all that you have discovered in yourself with them. Analyze all those feelings as closely as you can. And then replace your lover's name with [your yearning] or [your unlived parts]. Tell your partner honestly and openly about your desires and your unlived parts, your feelings and dreams.*

This is likely to take about as much courage as jumping off a cliff – but if you stick to your guns and disclose all your desires, dreams and fantasies, you will be amazed how much intimacy, vitality and freedom suddenly open up after this leap into fear and pain.

In love triangles, everyone's afraid of intimacy

The dilemma of a love triangle is always crying out for a courageous and honest declaration. It always involves three people who are avoiding taking their next major step towards healing and growth. All three (!!!) people involved are really being asked to confront, on their own, their fear of commitment and closeness.

A healthy relationship needs both partners to form a greater whole through constant openness and growth. If one of them represses old pain, doesn't express the fundamental and important parts of the relationship and doesn't allow new and risky developments to take place, the relationship is missing something. This 'empty' part works like a vacuum and creates a sucking pressure until it is filled – maybe by another person. Then the system is complete again, but still not intact. In love triangles it takes three people to add up to 100 per cent; two of them only add up to 50 or 60 per cent.

The third party embodies everything that the betrayed one isn't expressing. That person, of course, really doesn't want to know that the 'bad' third party might have something to do with them. They don't want to talk to them, don't want to argue with or be confronted by them – they just want them to go away. But this person has something that they are lacking – whether they want to know it or not. That is why I always encourage the cheated party to enter into an honest emotional discussion with the third party – who in turn is lacking everything that the cheated one embodies. Both are often completely out of balance, only in opposite directions.

The person in the middle should have entered into truthful communication and confrontation within the original relationship long ago. They should have led the way to new horizons, thrown all their old baggage overboard, inspired their partner and maybe the whole family with their patience and untiring involvement, day after day. Instead they ran away from responsibility, dreamed of ideal relationships, special partners and a different life, and were always chasing new rainbows.

Once a lover enters their life they say, 'This person is so special, so inspiring, so liberating and unique that they make me feel alive.' They don't recognize that it is the special circumstances that make them feel so alive. The really special, unique and inspiring thing is that – at least at the beginning – with this person they are living in the moment, without the baggage of old memories, bad experiences and entrenched demands. When talking about the highest state of being, every serious spiritual path ends in the Here and Now, in enlightenment in the present moment.

In our normal life, our familiar surroundings, our familiar relationship, we are hardly ever aware of the present moment. We avoid all sorts of things that we may once have experienced as bad or painful. We dream of all sorts of things that we hope to achieve, because that is where happiness lies. We have all sorts of ideas about how things should be. The result is that we plan our relationship to death and control away every bit of spontaneity. We paralyze each other with our fears and demands to the point where we feel safe, but then we are also cut off from all natural flow. We are no longer living with the person by our side but with our image of that person. The problem is, that doesn't do them justice.

Sometimes we can experience this game that our mind is playing with us, this quite amazing phenomenon, in fast forward with a lover. A woman came to me after she had had an affair and had returned to her husband. She had accidentally bumped into her former lover and had nearly burst out laughing. She had felt really embarrassed but at the same time enormously liberated. 'I must have been blind,' she said. 'I used to be absolutely convinced of how fantastically attractive he was. When I saw him again, it was as if the drugs had worn off. I saw a spindly, badly dressed Mister Average speaking with a strong accent that I have never liked. At one point I couldn't help myself – I just started laughing about all my old dreams.'

The marriage caterpillar and the butterfly lover

Re-establishing a truthful relationship with our partner works in exactly the same way as falling into a dream and then waking from it.

Chuck Spezzano has developed an almost magic recipe for love triangles and for notorious womanizers/man-hunters. Before Chuck started working with couples, he had been about a bit. He had changed partners more and more frequently until he had had to concede that this was getting him nowhere. None of the new partners seemed to be the right one and the novelty was wearing off more quickly each time. Often new and old relationships were overlapping. Eventually Chuck discovered that every new woman embodied the qualities that the last one didn't have. As soon as he started to long for those missing qualities, they seemed to turn up in his life – but in the shape of another woman.

Back then Chuck had not only been womanizing but had also been doing research into human consciousness and the power of the mind. He tried out a new strategy, with baffling results. He still focused his attention on what was missing in his relationship, but this time he believed with all his heart that it could be found *within* his current relationship. Instead of escaping, he got closer to the woman by his side and focused on the fact that everything he was missing was, in reality, right there. He was rewarded with a kind of miracle and turned this experience into an important strategy for healing relationships. It is simple: Give all your love, all your attention and curiosity back to your partner. Engage with them with all your heart and for a fortnight concentrate on the qualities that you are longing for. Believe that you will find them in your partner and your true partner will develop them.

For the last two decades Chuck has been happily married to the same woman. Together they work on healing relationships all over the world.

Everybody can take this path. Everybody can connect once more with the lost and isolated parts of their personality and believe in the power of their own love and their unlimited potential – and their partner's too. The magic word for this is 'commitment'. Commit yourself to reconnecting your heart and your sexuality. Work out what strategies you use to prove or maintain your independence. In reality you are simply distracting yourself from old heartbreak. Not being able to commit as adults is always about childhood traumas that never healed. And the longer we have shut off that old pain, the more courage it takes to finally show ourselves as the vulnerable beings that we are.

In love triangles, each of the people involved can set this urgently needed healing process in motion. Each of them can begin to recommit to their own truth and to stand up for it openly and courageously. Even someone who is being deceived and is not in the know will have an inkling that something is wrong in their relationship. But the one in the middle has the trump card with which they can take everybody else forward in one great leap. If they can disclose to their real partner that there is a third person in the relationship, this very pragmatic step will lead to much more clarity all round.

Often the one in the middle hesitates for a long time before confessing they have a lover. If this is you, I advise you to do it quickly. Only then can the journey begin towards the further growth that is so important for everybody involved.

In most cases the confession initiates conversations that should have taken place years ago. Often a lot of repressed and painful feelings break loose that nobody would have admitted to before. A person will often refuse to declare the identity of their lover. But in this case, too, I advocate telling the complete truth. Only when all the cards are on the table can everybody concerned move forward. As long as the lover is somehow kept secret, they will hold on to their place in the relationship in a powerful way. For that reason there is no greater challenge in healing a love triangle than to let go, to admit, to confess and to declare. For that reason, the question 'Which of the two is better for me?' keeps us away from the real task, which is 'Now I'm finally learning to make decisions and to commit myself totally and wholly to this one person!'

This path demands great commitment, openness and the courage to admit that you are vulnerable. It also demands something very old-fashioned: faithfulness and discipline. When you indulge yourself sexually, when you are forever looking for a new thrill and change your sexual partners frequently, you cannot take this path towards healing. Unfortunately, in this scientifically and technically orientated world we haven't a clue about deeper emotional and energetic contexts. We don't even suspect that a profound exchange of power occurs when two people who don't know each other very well just go to bed together, without the connection of love and trust. In this case, women use men rather like energetic vacuum cleaners to 'have a good clear-out', while men not only discharge their bodies but also their hearts.

Independence – worse than dependence

Stop being independent. Do you want to know what is worse than being dependent? Being independent, because it is a constant attempt not to be dependent. Commit yourself wholly to your partner.

By 'commitment' I don't mean sterile, dutiful faithfulness. Maybe you have been together for what feels like an eternity, but you daren't say how you really feel inside. The dreadful thing is that every unexpressed word, every muted feeling will build a wall between you and your partner and prevent deeper intimacy. That is why you play power games without admitting to it, why you fight for acceptance and attention. And, probably unconsciously, why you compete with each other. You want to be better than your partner so that they cannot hurt you. Be courageous and show your dependency and your fear. Your relationship can only be healed and transformed as a result.

The true healing of a person begins with an honest commitment to another person. The true healing of a love triangle lies in a deep desire for truthfulness and the courage to reveal that you are vulnerable. What follows is like a long walk through a desert full of hurt and new betrayal. The hard phase of openness and communication seems endless and tough. Time and again the thought of giving up will enter your head. Just as often you'll have the tempting idea that your ideal partner, your dream man or woman, is out there somewhere. But if you unwaveringly believe that your current partner can offer you everything that is needed for a fulfilling relationship, this will bring forward exactly those qualities in them. In this way the hole through which a third person can slip into the relationship will be filled in with truthfulness and life.

A while ago I had a wonderful experience. I had to go away on my own for a few days on business. I had an appointment with a man whom I had met twice before but didn't really know. We went out for dinner to discuss a few issues. I hadn't been in a situation like that in ages. After only a few moments there was something in the air. We were laughing as if we had known each other for a long time. We talked unusually openly and confidentially about work-related issues and challenged each other verbally. Fireworks were going off between us. I was in a wonderfully elated state which I really, really enjoyed. I felt at ease and feminine and apparently adored by this clever and attractive man.

That was all very wonderful and life-enhancing. But the really special thing was something different: I felt completely free to enjoy the attentions of this stranger. I was also able to talk openly to him about it. Was he aware of what was happening between us? He smiled and nodded. Without any warning I told him how much I liked his attentions. My openness took him by surprise. As if as a reward, he made me a few really flattering compliments. I also liked that very much and asked him whether he wanted to know why I was able to be so open with him. Yes, he wanted to know. I told him I could only feel so elated and free, so openly receptive to his attentions, because I felt so deeply connected to my husband.

The most wonderful feeling of all was that I did not have to feel shame or guilt about the fact that I could be open and feminine. And the man turned out to be exactly the right person for such an exciting encounter, because he understood immediately what I meant.

8

Separation – resolution is postponed

Separation and divorce have become everyday events. A recent study stated that since 1970 the divorce rate has risen by about one third. These days more or less every other marriage will end in divorce. The most frequent reasons are unfaithfulness, alcohol and violence, changes after the birth of the first child, arguments about money and people developing in different directions. Time and again I have talked about this to the people who come to me for therapy. Sometimes their stories are sad and resigned, sometimes bitter and cynical, sometimes incredibly dramatic. I have learned from all of them that whatever the reasons, and however painful and unforgivable they may be, separation is rarely is the solution. Separation is only shelving the real problem.

When men come to me I often compare a separation with a change of court in a tennis match. If a forehand always ends up in the net, the player won't solve the problem by changing the opponent or the court. The game won't get better on a new tennis court, with a new net or a new opponent, if a person is still using the same old overpowered forehand. In tennis there is only one solution for a long-standing problem shot: you have to retrain your responses, your tactics or your approach to the ball. But when the ball ends in the net all too often in our relationships, we try to change courts and find a new partner. We might find relief and new experiences when we do, but our game doesn't get any better. And eventually it all just leads to frustration and emptiness.

We hardly ever leave a relationship because we don't care about our partner. Mostly we leave – particularly when it isn't the first time – because we have given up. Because we don't know how to get the ball across the net any more. Because we don't know how to find a solution to something that we find unbearable. Often we have gone through the same painful sequence of events again and again, without the slightest hope of a change or resolution. It has drained the relationship and turned it into a battlefield. Finally, we feel that keeping our distance is the only way of avoiding getting hurt or choked any more.

Separation seems like salvation. At last we can breathe freely again. At last there is calm. The vicious circle has been broken. The pain diminishes. Separation is like being shipwrecked and then washed ashore on an island in the middle of the ocean. At last we have firm ground beneath our feet. But then, after a few moments of rest, when our wounds have closed and we have regained our strength, we look around – and if we are honest, we have to admit that we are stuck on an island. Sometimes there are two of us stranded there – us and the secret lover who was the apparent reason for the separation. Sometimes we are rescued very quickly by a new love we meet on the island. But whenever we want to return to the mainland – to our children, our families, our old friends and our everyday life – the ocean of old patterns and habits stretches out in front of us, and we have to cross it.

Separation as opportunity

Separation is not the answer to our problems. Eventually we will have to return to the point where our relationship got stuck so that we can look at it consciously and transform our part in it. If separation seems the only escape route, then at least we should make use of it on our way to personal growth and healing. If we look closely at it we might recognize its two major opportunities.

The first one is that taking such an abrupt step may force us into doing things that we either didn't dare do before or didn't give ourselves permission to do. If we do this consciously, we can grow and develop completely new skills and qualities.

Separation can also offer us space and time for recovery. By withdrawing and just being by ourselves for a while, without another person, we can heal our wounds, and our hearts can find peace again. Once we have regained our strength, all our old tasks and opportunities for development will still be there, waiting for us to tackle them on our way towards growth.

Maybe we left because our partner crossed our boundaries far too often. In this case separation re-establishes them. Sometimes divorce lawyers have to show us what rights and opportunities we have and explain that we have to fight for them. But at some point we will find that those rules only give us a reprieve. In the end we have to do the work ourselves. We have to learn to look after ourselves properly, to set boundaries and not say 'yes' when we mean 'no'. Otherwise it is only a question of time before we are confronted with the real issue – that the problem was not down to our former partner but the fact that *we* were not able to set boundaries.

No matter why we left – whether it was because our boundaries were ignored, we didn't get enough attention and support, we were lied to or cheated on, controlled or judged – for a while the separation ensures that we get what was lacking. Maybe it seemed to come out of the blue, maybe it was a threat that was finally carried out or maybe it came as a blessed relief. On closer inspection, separation always comes into our life to help us when we are not able to expand our own qualities and skills under our own steam. It occurs when we have lost the belief in finding a solution as a couple. It occurs when we have lost hope and don't feel able to rekindle our relationship. If we have arrived at such a dead end, where our pain seems unbearable and the paralysis insurmountable, then we have to work for a conscious and passionate separation – a separation from the heart.

A separation from the heart means that we consciously make use of the distance between us in order to become stronger and learn to accept our partner from this safe vantage-point. It might sound paradoxical, but we can only let go of resentment and grow when we make peace with our ex-partner. They have shown us our painful spots. They may have deepened our wounds, but they did not cause them. In many cases a separation, as I have said before, gives us the discipline to take the steps that we should have taken within the relationship but didn't. Separated mother hens automatically become confident women. Separated guest-fathers and visitor-husbands are, left to their own devices, challenged every weekend to be more responsible and empathic fathers. This way we are forced to honestly look at our limitations and to grow, even though we can only acknowledge this in hindsight. During this process of disentanglement, we find independence and also mutual respect – and we can practise getting our forehand reliably across the net.

Maybe you are contemplating a separation right now. Maybe you have separated already. Maybe you are in the process of entering a new relationship. This chapter is written with a single message that comes straight from my heart: like all the other aspects of a relationship, a separation, too, is ultimately only about one thing – learning how to love. It is the greatest challenge to our love, Afterwards, we won't need more from our ex-partner than they are able to give. We will be able to forgive them only to the degree that we have understood their behaviour. And we will only be truly free to form a new relationship if we have made peace with them and opened our heart again to them. Furthermore, it is only if we can let go of our ex-partners in true love that our children can find peace and stability and grow with adequate inner anchoring to their own male or female wholeness. (More about the impact of a separation on the development of children can be found in Chapter 14, 'Children of love'.)

Breaking free

'Love your ex-partner in order to let go of them...' Hardly ever has a sentence of mine met with such dismissal and protest as this one. Maybe you, too, are vigorously shaking your head. But there is only one way to find inner freedom as well as make an external break. The first step is to accept it. If you really want to be free of the old relationship, then you need to be at peace with it. And there is only one way to find real peace. In the end you won't have any other choice but to totally accept your old partner.

By this I don't mean to make you feel pushed back into the old relationship at any price. This is not about staying with your ex-partner. It is not about staying together at all costs.

Gloria came to me because she did not want a divorce. Her husband had left her for another woman. But Gloria categorically refused to accept the fact, let alone consent to a divorce. Her husband's battle against her became fiercer, the weapons more brutal. Every time Gloria's refusal to divorce was mentioned, she came back to the same point: the divorce of her parents. 'I always wanted to be a good example for my children,' she said. 'Part of a model couple that stayed together.'

During the course of our sessions, Gloria realized that her husband had actually been 'forced' to leave. It became clear that long before his affair their marriage had become a cliché that she had constructed for herself and it was a far cry from a vibrant partnership.

Gloria had never entered into an honest relationship – she had only shored her marriage up against a divorce. That is like saying: 'Don't think of a pink elephant now!' If you weren't thinking of a pink elephant before, you will be now. Likewise, if you need to stay together at all costs, then you will never be able to simply enjoy being together for the joy of it. Every attempt to stay together for an external reason – be it duty, responsibilities, children or friends – will paralyze your relationship. Love can never unfold under such pressure; you will never feel drawn towards your partner but will always feel unconsciously rejected. And your partner won't be able to develop a natural relationship with you either, because consciously or unconsciously they will feel used and pressurized. If, as in Gloria's case, the relationship has no inner strength and connection, there is no point in keeping it alive artificially. In such an empty shell of routine and duty you will dry out emotionally and at some point probably be confronted with exactly what you have been seeking to avoid – a separation.

This chapter is not about duty, role models, promises and staying together at all costs. It is about loving – even when we aren't with our partner any longer. 'And we are only truly free to form a new relationship if we have made peace with them and opened our heart again to them.' Maybe you are thinking now, 'Why should I love this person who has made my life so difficult?' I am not saying that you have to find your former partner wonderful. Loving someone doesn't mean being in love. It doesn't mean having to stay together. It doesn't mean adapting. It doesn't mean smiling when you want to cry. Love is the opposite of dependency. Love is free – it doesn't need anybody, it only wants to love. And loving means accepting what is.

Finding peace and freedom

In the context of a separation or divorce, acceptance means recognizing that the bad behaviour of your former lover had nothing to do with you. They weren't doing it just to hurt you or to deliberately deceive you. They might not have been able to satisfy your ideals and your needs. Maybe they had qualities that you didn't like or understand. They might have behaved in ways that you didn't appreciate and that you neither accepted nor respected. They might not always have responded to you as you would have liked them to. But the pain inside you doesn't stem from anything your former partner did. It arises because you couldn't accept it. Things became more and more intolerable because you resented and rejected the way your partner was. Now you have separated. But as long as you nag and scold, judge and despise, as long as you don't make peace with your former partner, you remain chained to them and their behaviour. You still want something from them – changes, corrections, attention. You still don't have enough.

'He was always at work!' This is the main reason women give for a separation. This complaint always sounds a touch condescending. In one case, Helen contemptuously called her very successful businessman husband and his partners 'big boys' or 'emotional cripples'. She said they were after money at all costs, they didn't have any real friends, they had no time for their families and their private lives, and they thought only of their career. Helen was searching for a more spiritual life, she was empathic and warm and had given up a promising career to look after the children. One day her husband had, apparently out of the blue, packed his suitcases and moved in with a considerably younger colleague, seemingly without any consideration for his wife and children. Even though he was very wealthy, he had not been willing to contribute voluntarily to their financial upkeep. Since then Helen had not only felt more righteous in every respect, but also *in* the right.

After the separation the only communication between Helen and her husband had been via solicitors. Helen had refused to communicate directly. She had also refused to allow her husband to come to their former home. By the time she came to see me, they weren't even speaking on the phone any more. The children were being handed over in a public space, a car park.

The more Helen's husband was distancing himself from the family and the less attention he was giving them, the more Helen was refusing to have contact. And the more she did this, the more stumbling blocks her husband put in place.

Helen said frequently that they had nothing more to talk about. She spoke of her former husband with cool contempt and described his behaviour with a superior smile. But when we went way back into her past, she was suddenly overwhelmed with guilt. Her heart had not been free when the relationship with her husband had begun. When she met him she had been deeply but unhappily attached to another man, and her husband had practically ripped her from his arms. During our talks Helen realized how long after the wedding she had been attached to the former partner and how little she had been available to her husband.

When talking about the future, Helen became very anxious and quiet. She had repeated visions of financial hardship and had to acknowledge that regarding the divorce, she was mostly interested in money. The moment she was forced out of the safe home where she had once been protected by her husband, she would fight for money in the same way that *he* had done all those years, along with all the other men in the business world that she despised so much. She also had to admit that behind her hard and silent front she was afraid of her husband and of further pain. Like him, she didn't show her feelings. She followed the strategy suggested by the divorce lawyers and also studied the law regarding her fight for justice and compensation – just as her husband had always done.

Eventually Helen recognized what countless women keep firmly repressed: she longed for status, power and money, but didn't believe that she was entitled to it. In that sense she felt just as worthless as all the men who, day in, day out, sacrificed their feelings and their private life for power and money. Whenever Helen condemned her husband, she was really condemning herself.

Learning to love and let go

Another woman I talked to during her divorce mentioned God. She was racked with guilt and afraid that God would condemn her for her increasingly bitter behaviour towards her husband during an increasingly bitter divorce. At one point I said, 'The greatest gift God has given you is your husband. Never before have you had such an opportunity to recognize yourself and learn to love yourself in spite of all your shortcomings. Never before have you had such a good chance to take a close look at your fears. Never before have you had so many opportunities to grow, to forgive another person and to let go.'

Since then I have told many people who are separating that their former lover, though currently the target of all their resentment, bitterness and anger, is the greatest gift they have ever had on their way to personal growth. They were heaven-sent – only not for the person to indulge in romantic love 'happily ever after' but for them to practise acceptance, true love and self-appreciation.

People often say they had to separate because of their partner's character and behaviour. We tend to say that we can only love someone when they are exactly the way we imagine they should be. We have probably been looking at ourselves in exactly the same way for a long, long time, whether consciously or not. And we dissociate ourselves from what doesn't come up to scratch.

Time and again we force ourselves to get things right for others, to conform and to adapt so that we are accepted and loved. When we project all this onto our partner and ask them to do or not to do or to be or not to be all sorts of things so that we can love them, that isn't love. It is more like control and dependency on certain behaviour. Most of all, this stance wordlessly implies that *we* need something, that *we* are lacking something in order to feel happy, safe and free. And it implies that only our partner can provide it.

This longing for a saviour, for someone who gives us what we need, is really a remnant from our childhood, when we were weaker and more helpless. Back then, when dealing with adults, we were painfully aware of our inferiority and power-lessness. We also experienced our behaviour being rejected and condemned. Physically we are adults now, but we still try to be nice and friendly to keep bad things at bay. We still look around for some kind of external power to heal our old wounds. We still carry our old fears of breaking down in the face of the loveless behaviour, the irresponsibility and the weakness of others. That is why we demand that they behave in a certain way – so that our old scars don't reopen. If they don't meet those demands, if they are incapable of soothing that recurrent pain, we unconsciously feel like powerless children again and are convinced that there is only one escape route. We have to leave that partner, we have to separate, we have to divorce them in order to regain our power.

Most people capable of a vibrant and lasting attachment have learned to behave independently of whether they feel loveable or not. They have learned to disconnect the behaviour patterns of others and their own need for attention from love. Love doesn't turn up because we are always nice and friendly. And it doesn't blossom when others bend over backwards to please us either.

If you really do need something to make you happy, it is self-discipline and the desire for development, growth and openness. If you really do need something to feel fulfilled, it is courage and consistency so that the unhappiness, the loneliness and the suffering which accompany this inner growth process can be endured. That is love. Love that allows you to realize your full potential. Love that develops compassion for the limitations of others. This love heals and sets you free – free from all the unhealed wounds of your earlier life, your dependency, your resentment, your bitterness and your eternal search for attention. The only true goal of love is spiritual growth. Separation offers a great opportunity to develop it.

'Until death do us part.' In these times of change, when society is constantly suggesting new needs and when nature is becoming increasingly volatile, this sentence might seem threatening. A lifelong attachment to just one person? We can hardly imagine it. And yet it is something we are all looking for. Our innermost being is searching for stable, enduring, deepening intimacy. At the same time it seeks the freedom to grow and fully unfold. That is a paradox. The acceptance of our own individuality is the only foundation on which a relationship can grow. The acceptance of a deep continuing attachment, especially when we want to get rid of it, makes us free for a loving separation. Therefore, separate from the heart – learn to love your former partner so you can truly let go of them.

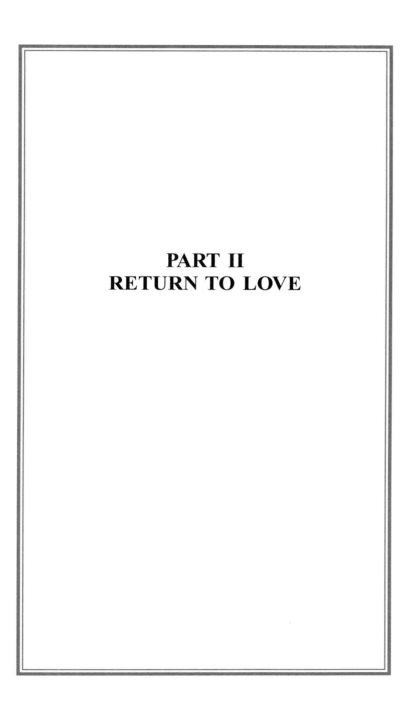

PART II
RETURN TO LOVE

9

True love — or the thing about God

Maybe you have read this far and are now feeling anything but optimistic in regard to your relationship. Maybe you have struggled dutifully through the last few chapters, with their countless attempts to make you feel grateful for all your partner's gloomy and energy-draining qualities, but without any real enthusiasm. Maybe those equally frequent admonitions that it is only down to you how your life pans out simply made you feel like giving up. Maybe you feel like the man who was dragged into my office one day by his wife. He explained his reluctance with the words: 'I've been to couples therapy with my wife before. Now I know everything there is to know about me, and about her. And I know even more clearly why I want to divorce her.'

Everything I have written about relationships so far might sound like a tunnel without an exit to you. There are so many painful issues from the past that we can hardly hope to track down them all. And as no one else is faring any better, we'd better stop hoping for a prince or princess to turn up. All we can be certain of is that we are all carrying a whole bundle of hurts around with us, that we hardly know our partner, that we are all more or less commitment-phobic and that complete happiness is a mirage.

There's no hope in sight. Love and romance, a passionate affair, the dream woman, the ideal man, the secret lover, even a divorce – every option in a relationship sooner or later leads to the same problem: somebody else seems to be responsible for our happiness or unhappiness. When we feel attached, full of love and acceptance, it is only because we have found the right person. But when the relationship doesn't work out, it is, of course, because that person didn't turn out to be the right one. We feel bad because they did this or that. How perfect our lives would be if only they would change! How often have we come to that conclusion?

The truly bizarre thing in this very common thought process is that the *other person* seems to be lacking something that *we* need in order to feel better. We are afraid of it, we long for it, we miss it and need it – and it is our partner who is responsible or to blame. When arguments and attitudes start hardening, our view becomes even more distorted. Then we even claim that *we* are right and our partner is wrong. Their very existence becomes the reason for our suffering and our shortcomings. We believe firmly that they are guilty of everything. Their behaviour is what we have to challenge, confront and, if necessary, escape from.

Now this is really mad, but it is not only generally accepted as absolutely normal but also vehemently defended if it is ever questioned. So, a really important step towards personal peace is to learn to question our own thinking and to let the real truth seep in: no matter what we do in this world, there is nothing that can *bring* us peace and fulfilment. There is nothing *out there* that can free us from our unhappiness, our emptiness, our searching and our pain – no partner, no relationship, no success, no possessions. Any attempt to find Mr or Ms Right only leads us further away from our real opportunities to discover our true path. In the words of a wise man, all that we can find by searching is another search.

Remember the opening words of this book? 'I know that it can work out. I know that your relationship can be just what you want it to be.' I still claim that's true. It can work out. Of course it can. But in all probability not in the way you imagine it. It will require a complete reversal of your usual view of the world – which means a kind of quantum leap.

The thing about God

There is this thing about God. I can't keep it from you, even though I know from many talks with clients how confusing and how loaded with fear and shame this issue is. In our society, faith, prayer and God seem to be taboo for a great number of people. It seems too dangerous to risk losing your foothold in the realm of the undefined, the unknowable, the scientifically unproven. But could you try it just for a moment...?

With my background I have not exactly been God's PR manager from birth. In my family there were, however, numerous discussions about faith and the church. At one point, all my family left the church at once, even though it meant that within our provincial and strictly Catholic environment we were looked upon as pariahs. Later in life I was quite proud of this rebellious spirit in my genes and for a long time declared myself an atheist. Until one day the thing with God sneaked into my life again unexpectedly and spread in such a way that today I can claim that God is the solution to all my problems.

No matter how much I struggled against it at first, in my search towards fulfilment I always ended up with God. However, I was able to realize that this was more of a conscious concept than the man with a long white beard of my childhood confessions. For me, God isn't embodied in any specific religion and I won't necessarily meet him in church rather than at the hairdresser's. But the power God represents is, for me, the answer to the whole question of relationships.

I have come to the conclusion that when we really want to enjoy an honest and fulfilling relationship, we have to be willing to delve down into the very depths of our being. There, at our innermost core, we are all ultimately spiritual beings, even though society persists in calling us consumers first and foremost. Looking at the people who come to me in their search and at society as a whole, I believe that our personal and collective evolution is inevitably moving towards realization of this insight, in spite – or even because – of our rapidly increasing information and communication overload.

C. G. Jung said that of all his patients who were past their midlife, that is, older than 35, there was not a single one whose ultimate problem was not one of religious belief. Everybody was ultimately suffering from having lost what living religions had always given their followers. And no one could really be healed if they couldn't regain their religious belief.[1]

My clients have taught me that faith is the greatest healer of them all. Most people who come to me are between their mid-

....

1. C. G. Jung, *Zur Psychologie westlicher und östlicher Religionen* (Vol. II), Olten, 1971

thirties and mid-forties – people on the cusp of their lives. Fewer and fewer of them find fulfilment in the 'normal' concept of life based on external things. Most of my clients have had a good education, years of personal development, a career and worldly success. Many of them have achieved a great deal but not found what they have been looking for – meaning and fulfilment. They have walked the path which in our society is signposted at every corner: the path to self-realization via status, career, knowledge, wealth and success. But none of their attempts to be acknowledged just as they were has given them lasting fulfilment.

Once they escape from this cul-de-sac and end up with me – often involuntarily – those people often feel a diffuse and inexplicable fear. They are anxious because they have not managed to make their life really meaningful. They feel helpless because nothing that they have achieved or acquired has given them real contentment. Nothing has supported their sense of self-worth. Quite the opposite – many describe feeling under constant pressure, perpetually driven and unable to get absorbed in anything or to find peace anywhere. Everything seems to be constantly changing and, worse, more and more demands are being made all the time.

The senselessness of victory

We have hardly pulled ourselves up to the next rung of the career ladder when the next challenge is waiting for us. We have barely completed a marathon before we want to improve our record. As soon as the latest software has been installed on our computer, there is an update with even more features. As soon we have starved ourselves to a size 12, we meet a friend who is a size 10. We have reached management level, but then there is the board, and anyhow the banks make the decisions now. We have finally amassed enough property and possessions, but then we start worrying that we might lose them all again.

Everywhere new dangers are lurking and new improvements can be made, there are always people who are more important and more powerful than we are, and something bigger and more beautiful keeps turning up, either in our imagination or right in front of our eyes. Nothing ever seems enough to give us lasting contentment. Not even our latest husband, our new mistress or our secret affair. There seem to be more and more opportunities to satisfy our desires, but they turn out to be as tasteless as tinned tomatoes.

Many people feel completely drained by this chase for fulfilment, this feeling of being constantly driven, always having to do something in order to be or to get something. If we let religion back into our lives, it gets a lot easier. Then we don't have to do everything ourselves. We don't have to overburden our partner with our needs either. No matter whether we adhere to a particular faith or assume a divine, complete, peaceful and spiritual core as the centre of our being, we can rely on the fact that there is something beyond us, that we are connected to a higher power and a higher force, that something is flowing towards us and guiding us, and that there is something that is giving to us. This concept brings us immediate relief and takes a large burden off our partner's shoulders.

If we expect to get everything from our lover, we should turn towards faith. The best thing religion is capable of is reconnecting us to love – and thereby to God. God is not an abstract concept but a loving presence. If we believe in God, we are connected to a loving force that holds us in its embrace. The concept of God is all-embracing. God is all-embracing love. If we are connected to God, we are part of a universal higher entirety. The laws of the universe say that macrocosms are like microcosms. The whole, in its being, corresponds to the smallest part. The smallest part, in its being, corresponds to the whole. If we are connected to God, our inner core is divine. If we are connected to a divine presence by religion or spirituality, our core being is constantly receiving and we can in turn pass this on and give to others.

This is not simply a theory, a church doctrine for Sunday mass; it's more of a deepening connection to God that brings about real changes in everyday life. If God is not a separate almighty figurehead who judges or praises us, who makes us confess to our sins and suffer for them or who generously absolves us, if it is rather the basic essence of being, if it is an all-embracing and ubiquitous loving presence and we are part of it, then it follows that our core being is wonderful and divine too. Then there must be something in us, underneath all our pain, our confusions and tribulations, that is utterly beautiful and loveable. Then in our lives there will also be things that are beautiful and loveable. Then every moment in our life is only about one thing: do we want to acknowledge this eternal power in us or not? Do we turn to the divine presence inherent in us or not?

If we do allow ourselves to open up to this concept – even if at first with doubt and a lot of rational analysis – it could revolutionize our sense of ourselves, our relationships and our lives. Searching for this all-embracing love, we begin to look at ourselves and begin to be gentler with ourselves. We want to understand ourselves. We become more attentive and aware of our heart's desires and dreams. We take our own needs more seriously. We begin to think that maybe we're fine after all, just as we are. We don't have to rush around any more in a constant search for someone or something that will give us whatever fills our aching emptiness. We learn to accept ourselves and, step by step, can fall back on ourselves, delve deeply into our innermost selves and give to others, just because we enjoy doing it. We can rest in ourselves. We can become authentic.

We don't have to do anything

When she was young my daughter always wanted a prayer before going to bed at night. Sometimes I pinched her little finger, saying, 'This is you – and God is your whole body. If He moves, you move too.' Later we tried pinching all her toes, her hair, her navel, her earlobes and her nose to see whether they were parts of God. Yes, even her raised middle finger – she found that one particularly amusing. In a way it all boils down to one thing: if we allow a loving divine presence to enter us, we allow ourselves to receive. We don't have to do anything for this – we are just like a little cell. We are part of this body, we live in it and are nurtured by it.

Just stop for a moment. Let yourself absorb this image of a little cell which is part of a greater whole. Take a deep breath and try to feel your body from the inside out. Imagine you are this small cell. Pay attention to how your breath is flowing in and out of your chest and your abdomen. Be aware that your breath is always flowing, whether you pay attention to it or not. It comes and goes, in and out, as reliably as the ocean waves washing around your toes on the beach. In truth, your breathing breathes you. And it doesn't only breathe you, but everything else that is alive at this moment. The same air that is entering you right now also enters me. At this moment we are connected. You are a little cell. I am a little cell. Every time I consciously pay attention to my breath I am fascinated by this image. What if we really are only a tiny cell of the liver, bone or skin of the universe? What if we are suffering from amnesia and have forgotten this universal connection? What if we only think that we are lonely, separate beings? What if we are a part of everything that is?

Pay attention to your breath. It is flowing. Whether you are aware of it or not, it is flowing. All the time. It is moving your body, opening and closing it. It is nurturing you. It is keeping you alive. Try to stop it. You will only manage for a short time. Then it will penetrate even more deeply into your lungs.

Breathing is such a normal activity that we are hardly ever conscious of it, but it is one of the great mysteries of life. It *is* life. And in my view it is our divine connection. But in order to be aware of this constant source of life and movement in our body, to recognize its true divine presence, we have to allow ourselves a moment of silent contemplation.

If we allow ourselves to experience this silence, we will experience the loving creature that we are deep inside. If we nurture this truth for a while, it will also manifest itself clearly in the rest of our lives. Once we are more at ease with ourselves and start to sense our own authority, we can let go of our roles, our addictions and social demands. We can slowly become more authentic. We can simply allow ourselves to be the way we are. We can allow ourselves to express what we feel. We can trust in the abundance of life and respond to our true calling.

The more deeply we go back to our own roots, the more clearly we can sense how deeply connected we are to others. The more we are at ease in ourselves, the more we become aware that we only fight, complain, reject, desire and crave in those places where we can't be ourselves any more. Only when the connection to our inner greatness has been lost are we in conflict with or in need of others around us. We learn that it is we who need to pay attention to all the places that are hurting inside. Whenever we approach something with such an attitude, we can give and receive love and support without hesitation. We don't have to reject other people's weakness resentfully, but can see behind it their search for love, for their own divine core, their connection to a greater power.

With time, our whole sense of being will change. We will experience self-worth. We will realize that we need less and have more to give. The more we are involved with ourselves, the more we will be aware of this all-embracing divine presence. The more we trust in this inner connectedness, the more we will find that the love flows from inside us. The more we understand that every one of our actions, our thoughts, our words, is invigorated by this presence, the more we will go through life with trust. I call this feeling 'It'll be OK!'

Maybe you have felt touched by the last few paragraphs. Maybe something inside you has remembered the truth in those words. Maybe you are just shrugging them off with the thought: 'Sounds quite convincing... She puts it quite nicely – but I don't sense anything like that in myself.' What I am talking about is a path. Even though at the moment you might not feel like taking it, it will unfold in front of you if you are willing to take the first small step. You just have to be willing to walk forward, even though you don't know how. The rest happens automatically. This might sound really strange, but it's true. As a former atheist, always searching and full of doubt, I could never grasp this logically. But one day I simply experienced it.

If at the moment you don't believe in any gods in this world, if you don't think there's anything to what I've just described, if you doubt whether your life could ever develop in this way, but if from the bottom of your heart you want to belong and to feel alive, then all you have to do is to say 'yes' to yourself. I assure you that if you do, your life will change and your relationship will heal. Maybe it will happen in an obvious and dramatic way, maybe gently and quietly, but you can be sure that nothing will ever be the same again.

This path is nothing you can prepare for and has nothing to do with theories, methods and approaches. Those things may give us an idea or point us in a certain direction, but in the end the path leads to our own personal 'It'll be OK' feeling. It is a path that life places us on quite naturally. Everything that happens to us, everything that touches us, everything that we encounter, is exactly what we need on our journey. No matter what your life looks like at the moment, it is the best it can be for your growth. It is tailor-made just for you. I don't know how often I have heard a person say, after the deep and painful process of working through a relationship: 'If he hadn't cheated on me I would never have learned...' or 'If she hadn't chucked me out I would never have woken up...' At the moment of crisis everything seems wrong, but in hindsight those deep wounds were the best thing that could have happened to us.

Every journey is unique. It is never the same for any two people. Everybody meets their own challenges, obstacles and bottlenecks on the way. And, paradoxically, they are the things pointing us in the right direction. Each of our problems has a hidden gift for us. Every time we conquer an addiction, challenge a fear, heal a disease, master a crisis, survive an accident, forgive our partner or our parents, we immediately gain new strength. No authority, no leader can show us how to do this or supply us with this strength. If we are really looking for fulfilment, we have to trust in our own leadership. We have to trust in the fact that we are fine as we are, no matter how painful or difficult our life is at the moment. We need those obstacles and hindrances in order to realize that we possess the resources necessary to overcome them. We have to learn that we have more power than our fear has made us believe. We have to discover that miracles can happen and that in utterly bleak situations the universe will come to our aid. We have to know that our prayers are being heard.

But no church, no temple, no seminar, no missionary and no book on relationships will be able to connect us to this faith in God and our own divine core unless we are willing to enter into it. When we are ready, we don't actually need any mediators or persuasion. Mostly, though, we are only truly willing when we have lost all faith in mediation, lost all our convictions and aren't listening to anybody any more. For the most part, our life has to be skirting the abyss of complete meaninglessness and despondency before we are able to truly open up and ask for help. It is usually only when we're in a complete crisis, when we feel we've lost all control over our life and are questioning our strengths and beliefs, that we are finally able to surrender ourselves.

God's not an old man with a grey beard

Even when we don't want to see God, He can show Himself to us. Personally, I never wanted to be involved with God. That is why it took a long time and some dramatic events before I recognized God for what He really is. Before that, I had caught a glimpse of Him several times. Each time involved a confrontation with death. Once I was caught in a shoot-out in

South Africa and a bullet only missed me because a black stranger pulled me under a car and saved me. I have also survived three car crashes in miraculous ways. Each time I was sure I was going to die, only to crawl out from under the wreck a few minutes later. Every time I experienced the same phenomenon. When I thought it was all over, for a brief moment I was flooded with a sense of incredible peace. Then as soon as I realized that I was going to get out of it alive, it disappeared and was replaced by great anxiety.

My last experience of being at death's door took place in slow motion. I had been on a skiing holiday. On the way home our bus took the high and winding roads through the Swiss Alps. Suddenly there was a smell of burning rubber. Somebody was just cracking a joke about the brakes failing and us all crashing down into the ravine when one of the drivers jumped up, pulled on the handbrake and shouted: 'Everybody down!' The brakes were indeed failing.

The bus was going faster and faster, and panic spread among the 40 or so passengers. Some shrieked, others whimpered, some threw themselves on the floor, others froze. I couldn't move and remained in my seat as if glued to it. I saw cars coming towards us, trying to veer around the bus. It was like a James Bond movie. I watched, completely paralyzed, but in my head there were a clarity and calmness I had never felt before in my life. We tackled two minor bends and then raced towards a hairpin bend that we would never manage to get round. It was as if everything inside me was relaxing, well, dissolving, while I was waiting for death, that deep ravine still visible out of the corner of my eye. Then there was a bump, a crash and a dull thud. Inside my head there was an incredible peace and a silence I had never experienced before.

A short time later it came to me, as though through a soft-focus lens, that things around me were chaotic. Everybody was trying to escape from the smouldering wreck. The bus had come to a standstill only a few inches in front of a house, and none of the passengers had suffered serious injury. It was a miracle. On the side of the bend which we would not have been able to corner was a low wall that had broken the speed of the bus. Behind the wall was a woodshed, which again had slowed the vehicle down, but which had disintegrated in the process. Behind the woodshed was a house, the first floor of which was projecting at head height. This had caught the top of the bus and brought it to a standstill.

Under normal circumstances I can't bear the sight of blood, but for a long while, as if in a trance, I busied myself helping the injured in a quiet and unthinking manner. It was as if I was walking on clouds and I had a sense of infinite strength and compassion. Eventually, though, I looked down my body and saw blood everywhere. Abruptly I awoke from my trance-like state. It was like suddenly being defrosted in a microwave. Tears came streaming down. I was frightened, my teeth were chattering and I collapsed with exhaustion.

I have never been able to forget that feeling of absolute peace that ended so abruptly. But at the time I never connected it to God or anything else. Every time I remember it now I feel deeply grateful. What also remained with me was a newly won certainty that even the most unimaginable is indeed possible.

It's only today that I know that at that moment – and also at the other times of crisis – I met God. In the face of death I could let go of everything, could abandon myself completely and relax to such a degree that I was able to feel the deep peace, the indescribable compassion and the love filling my innermost core. I could experience the certainty that miracles can happen and that help can come in the bleakest situations. It took a few more extreme situations in my life before I could really take it on board, though. Only with patient and relentless support from the universe was God slowly able to sneak into my life.

Some years later I was in a really bad state both professionally and privately. I had had a nervous breakdown and withdrawn from everybody. A friend of mine had sent me an English book with a fitting title about some messengers of dusk. When I opened the parcel I thought, 'Bound to be some spiritual nonsense... I wish she would stop bothering me with stuff like this.' Apart from that, I found reading it in English too demanding at the time, and so it ended up in a corner. Within the next two weeks, for inexplicable reasons it dropped on my toes three times. The third time I cursed, opened it and said grumpily, 'What the hell do you want from me?' Hours later, after reading about fate, guidance and universal laws, I was left with the strange feeling of not having understood a thing, but somehow having known it all already. It was as if I had found something I'd lost or forgotten a long time ago. I suddenly had an inkling that there was something higher, something greater, something more than there was in my fairly empty life.

Dying to be reborn

But my real baptism of fire came years later. My baby didn't want to be born – even though I was incredibly well prepared for it. The birth of my child was to be the most gentle, baby-friendly experience ever. I had everything prepared like a military exercise. I had read everything that could possibly be found in the bookshops nearby. I had done relaxation and breathing exercises with the baby inside me. I had played music and found a wonderful doctor and a gentle midwife. But my baby didn't want to be born. The date had long gone, but I was determined to leave it to nature. The doctor urged me to have it induced. I refused, but one day the monitor showed signs of complications for the baby. The labour was induced and it overwhelmed me with the force of an earthquake. For a day and a night I had the strongest contractions, but still my baby didn't want to come out. By then I was only a shadow of my former self, so the doctors recommended a Caesarean. But I had been so determined to do it all naturally...

I had rejected an epidural several times – also because of wanting it all to happen naturally – but by noon the next day I was crying out for one. But by now my body was in such a state that the anaesthetic wouldn't work. Eventually the doctor refused to take responsibility if I wouldn't agree to a Caesarean. With my last bit of strength I consented and surrendered to fate. For the first time I truly did let nature take its course. And again something happened which had happened so often before in my life. Something inside me relaxed. I became calm and just let things happen. And in the cold, tiled and clinical operating theatre, the last place I would've expected it, I met with so much love. Lying on the operating table in the knowledge that my baby would not enter this world 'naturally', another little miracle happened. One doctor held my hand while my husband stroked my forehead, another doctor gently talked to me and the nurses smiled until I cried tears of happiness, and said, 'It'll all be OK.' Then I passed out.

When I came round again, the doctors and nurses were standing around my bed and my husband was holding our daughter, blissfully smiling. They all stared at me silently, while I heard myself saying over and over again, 'I am dead. I am dead.' It took another hour before I had my baby at my breast and finally realized that I was alive and so was my daughter. My husband and the nurses told me later that while I had still been under the anaesthetic, I had been smiling and telling the most astounding stories about being dead, about light and peace and love.

Again I had had to surrender completely. I had had to give up every one of my plans, had had to die in order to give birth. I had been determined to let things take their natural course, but further ultrasound investigations revealed that my lovely daughter's thick skull would never have passed through the birth canal. A so-called 'natural birth' would have meant serious complications. Nature, and my baby, had been much cleverer than me and all my plans. Once more I was filled with deep gratitude. For the first time I tentatively asked myself whether there might be something like a divine force in my life. But this time the feeling wasn't to last either. I quickly forgot the thought.

It took one more serious crisis before my first inklings that there was a higher force worth believing in turned into a feeling of trust that my life was protected by God. I owe my final and greatest change to the bleak state of my marriage. It was my loneliness and the desolation of my relationship that threw me back onto myself and, through that, towards God. There was nothing spectacular about it, no great shock, no sudden encounter with death. It was a slow sickness that ate me up inside, a silent, gnawing feeling that something was lacking in my life. Week after week, month after month, loneliness settled in me and made me feel very uneasy. But I didn't dare to talk about it to other people. I was newly married and had a baby – I should have been happy. But I wasn't happy – I was terribly unhappy! Then one evening I was standing on our patio and I began to pray. I was actually quite shocked when I heard myself praying loudly to God. I asked for help and cried quietly. Then I went to bed on my own, because my husband was away again. But I didn't feel as lonely as I had the night before. And so I prayed more often.

What my prayers led to would take up the last hundred pages or so of this book. I won't go into all that here. However, it is my hope and belief that the things I'm saying in this book will touch some people deeply enough to inspire them to get in touch with their own spiritual core. I hope that you will also leave behind the loneliness of your relationship or the desolation of your life and dare to enter into this strange and powerful process which I dived into as if into a maelstrom. By opening yourself to the truth described here, you will find the truth will come to you too. It is nothing that you can make happen. But it may disclose itself to you while reading this, and then you will simply know it. And eventually you might just begin to feel that things will work out. Maybe...

Let me tell you my favourite story. A man had a dream. He dreamed that he was walking along a beach with God. In the sky, scenes from his life were being played back. And for each scene from his life there were footprints in the sand. When he looked back on the tracks, sometimes he saw two sets of prints, then only one. In times of great need and grief, he noticed there was only one. So he said to the Lord, 'Lord, I have noticed that during the sad times in my life only one set of footprints is visible. But you promised to be always with me. I don't understand why you left me on my own when I needed you most.'

And the Lord answered, 'My dear friend, I love you and would never leave you. During the days when you suffered most and needed me most and where there is only one set of footprints, I carried you.'

10

Honestly, there are lies in your marriage

Now, how can you find this path to self-realization in everyday life? How can you find God and your 'It'll be OK' feeling? How can you really be your true self and rediscover the all-embracing, loveable presence in yourself? How can your life come alive again? How can the frog by your side turn into a prince or princess? How can your marriage become an adventure again?

Just stop and stand still – right where you are. You don't have to do anything, you don't have to change anything – just be in the Here and Now of your life right now. Sit down and look at everything as if you'd never seen it before. Be as curious as a stranger who has no idea what your life is like. The most difficult part of this is being honest. This is not about concepts, approaches, ideas or images of your life – this is about how you *really* feel inside.

So what is your life like? Aren't you very keen on it any more? Do you find your wife boring? Are you afraid your husband might be having an affair? Do you yearn for your lover while you are surrounded by your family? Has anybody any idea of how lonely you are? Do you sometimes think, 'If only people knew...'? Are you carrying out your duties, including your marital duties, like a robot? Are you escaping into all sorts of wild and hyperactive distractions? Are you withdrawing emotionally and only going through the motions? Are you the best and most successful person around but still empty inside? Have you achieved nearly everything but found it has no meaning for you? Has anybody any idea about how you feel?

Sometimes we'd rather die

I once spent a terrible evening with a friend of mine who had invited us over. Everything was perfect – the other guests, the food, the table decorations – but the atmosphere was wrong. Something was in the air. That evening, when all the other guests had left and my friend's husband and children had gone to bed, she and I stayed up talking for ages. She was desperate; she felt hollow inside. She felt bitter, helpless and utterly neglected by her husband. She confessed that her marriage was unbearable. As the hours passed she spoke more and more openly of her loneliness, her fear and her depression. In the end she said that she suspected her husband of having an affair and that she often thought about taking her own life. She couldn't go on like this – no way.

When we finally went to bed I couldn't sleep at all. I felt numbed by the idea that her life was such a sham. I knew her as a person who was always active, always planning holidays, parties or visits. She was the sort of person whose notice-board was covered with invitations. When I had met her, more than 20 years ago, she had been a confident and popular girl, with men falling at her feet. Now she was beautiful, talented, had several children, was a pillar of society...

I couldn't sleep for worrying about what I should do. I knew her well enough to know how resilient and strong she could be when she had to. And she had wanted this life, after all. She had had a clear picture of her ideal life and, over the years, bit by bit, had put it together like a jigsaw puzzle. And now, as it was taking shape and had become exactly the way she had wanted it to be, she was finding that it didn't make her feel the way she had expected it to. But I knew that she would not simply let go of it all.

When I came down the next morning, her husband was sitting at the kitchen table and the children were larking about. I felt exhausted from lack of sleep and worrying about my friend, and greeted her sadly and with pity. She was whizzing around, sent the children into the garden to play and chirped, 'Good morning, honey! Did you sleep OK? It's a wonderful day!' It was as if I had had a nightmare – as if I had been with another person the previous night, as if those desperate hours had never happened.

That morning all my attempts at honesty failed. My friend served breakfast for her husband, organized the children's day and their upcoming schedule and pretended that nothing had happened. She had a clear concept of her life and she would not give it up easily. But truth is the only thing that really heals. The biggest problem my friend had was not that her marriage was on the rocks but that she had not been able to acknowledge that sad truth to herself and others.

Do you know the kind of state where your inner world and your external life are so far apart that it feels like doing the splits untrained, all the sinews stretched close to breaking point? I believe that most people in long-term relationships experience such a strong emotional split time and again. We have an image of our life, with the people around us as the parameters, and everything that doesn't fit into the framework we hide from ourselves, from our partner and our friends. Our need to feel connected to others is so strong that we are unconsciously prepared to sacrifice our very life for it. My friend preferred to accept her inner death and to torture herself with suicidal thoughts rather than voice her real needs to her family and her surroundings.

Lies for love

Sometimes things are really boring. We don't feel like chatting to our neighbour and make the excuse that we have to take the children to gymnastics now. Sometimes it is more difficult: we build houses, drive cars and arrange to see people that are important for our status or our career but who don't mean that much to us. Sometimes it becomes downright existential. We earn a lot of money, but we can't sleep. Sometimes it robs us of our mind. Sometimes we only make love to our partner out of duty and afterwards feel empty and used.

The bad thing is not that we do all this – it's only human. The tragic thing is that we try to hide our inner fears from ourselves and everybody else. We do it to stay in our relationship, of course, to go on being loved and avoid being deserted. But we achieve exactly the opposite. Since we are afraid of not being loved for ourselves, we present a false front, but in return we only receive a fake response. With every role we play, every friendly lie we tell, we become even more unhappy. We don't show how we feel; we don't say what we think. We turn our whole life into a lie, and sometimes it can become so unbearable that we actually want to take our own life.

My friend's life and marriage matched her idea of what she wanted but not what her heart really desired. Our ideas are always shaped by outside expectations, by our families, our conditioning, our inadequacies and our society, but only our heart knows our real needs. To express hers, my friend would have had to let go of a lot of control, draw firmer boundaries and show helplessness and weakness... But it would have been better for her if she had. She should have entered into an honest uncompromising dialogue with her husband and her surroundings about her heart and her true nature. She should have turned the night she shared with me into her own day.

Initially, this process is never pleasant. Once we dare to start it by stepping out of our cosy comfort zone, it often feels as though we are overwhelmed by a deluge that rips everything apart – regardless.

Endings come before beginnings

I have experienced such a deluge in my life. My husband was due to celebrate a milestone birthday and having a party was important to him. It was to be a real reunion: he had invited friends from all over the place. Everything was to be particularly special for the occasion – tasty food, lovely surroundings – but eventually those exaggerated expectations only made my own dismal state look even more dismal.

When the day came, he was at work and I was in the kitchen, busy with the preparations, when I suddenly felt as though I was being choked. Yet again he was away, as he had been so often during the last few months. Yet again I had been left alone to run our entire domestic life. Yet again I had to put on a good show in front of his friends while nobody had any idea of how I really felt. Yet again I had to be the perfect hostess, while all I wanted to do was run away.

I put the food out, lit the candles, prepared the drinks and forced myself into a dress, all the while close to tears. Only moments before my husband and the guests were due to arrive, I felt a feeling of helplessness rising in me, coupled with an almighty wrath. Then my husband and the first guests arrived. 'Hello!' Kiss, kiss. 'Long time no see!' I tried to function as I had so many times before, tried to play the gracious hostess. But it didn't work. I had to escape to the kitchen to calm the bursting volcano inside me. At one point a friend came in and said, 'Hey, what's the matter?' Then it was as if a hole had been blasted in a dam. I burst into tears and sobbed words that I wasn't even conscious of: 'I have to get a divorce! I have to get a divorce! I can't go on like this!'

Everybody remembers that birthday party. Some guests we never saw again. Others still share a laugh with us. My eruption in the kitchen, my withdrawal to the bedroom, the rumours of a divorce – all that spread like a thunder cloud over the party. My husband could only save himself from my deluge by drowning his sorrows. The next day, when he had sobered up and all the guests had left, nothing in our marriage was the same.

I said everything I had to say – things I had long ceased to have the courage for. He told me that he was seeing another woman. I told him I had wanted to leave him for a long time. We were both empty and resigned to the situation, but at the same time afraid to actually make the break. So often I had thought it all over in my head and had found hundreds of reasons why things couldn't go on as they were. But I couldn't see any way out.

Once we let go, healing begins

There were always two alternatives. Either I stayed and slowly shrivelled up like a plant without water or I destroyed my family and gave up on my dream of trying to achieve something with my husband that I had never managed with anyone else. I felt that I was slowly being ripped apart – and finally I could not bear the tension any longer. I was forced to let go. I could do no more analyzing, blaming, understanding and rationalizing. I sat down in front of my husband and everything simply flooded out – all my feelings, my fears, my secrets, my desires and my wish to divorce. I talked and talked until the stream dried up – and all at once I could look at him openly, dry-eyed. And then something completely absurd happened. For the first time in an eternity I felt in touch with myself and in touch with my husband. There was a deep silence between us and then a strange, calm feeling of truthfulness and belonging – a feeling that neither of us had experienced for years, a hint that maybe things could work out after all...

What a nightmare we had had to go through before we had managed to regain this feeling! But neither of us had voluntarily made the move before. It had taken an enormous build-up of pressure to get us started. We had had to talk about divorce first. It's often only when we are in crisis that we are really willing to listen to our soul. When people come to me at the height of a personal crisis I often hear them say; 'I can't go on. I don't see any way out. Sometimes all I want to do is die.' They see their crisis as a disaster without a solution. In their mind, though, such a breakdown is a relief – a liberation of the true self from the prison of demands and concepts. At last there is space for truth and for our true feelings to flow.

Even though society doesn't tell us so, our body and mind are simply servants of our soul. Our soul wants to express itself through them, because this is how it can show its true self. The soul's little voice is easily overlooked, but it is our true leader. Unfortunately our body and mind are often buried under the concrete slab of our goals and targets so there is no room left for the tender trickle of our soul. It is like choking from inside, being blinded and deafened to our own calls. We cannot feel our soul any more. We are absorbed by everyday demands and are rarely able or willing to listen to its voice or to even follow it. We have a plan, we have an image and we have demands. But our soul is always seeking the realization of our true self, our full potential and our personal growth. Its only aim is the unfolding of our complete and divine being. And it does not matter to our soul how successful, intelligent or socially acknowledged we are.

Why disasters are useful

Sometimes we get ourselves into situations that seem catastrophic, but they force our soul to develop and push it towards an unfolding of our perfect inner being. When we lose a loved one, our job, our home or our health, we experience fear and frustration. But from the viewpoint of our soul we are experiencing a healing crisis, an opportunity for growth.

After that disastrous but truthful birthday party my husband and I had to admit to each other that there was no way our relationship could carry on. We decided to go our own way for a while and live our own lives. It was a wordless, painful and lonely phase, but at the same time extremely honest and healing. We were faced with a heap of rubble that we had stumbled over countless times before without acknowledging its existence. For ages we had unconsciously been aware of it, but we had kept silent about it and tried to act out our marriage right next to it. Now that the wounds were ripped open we both began to start clearing up the rubble from our respective corners, the parts we felt responsible for. We only realized much later that the birthday party had been a new beginning for our marriage.

Life is so much cleverer than we are. If we hold back, if we avoid looking at what's right in front of us, if we don't listen to our heart even though every day we sense more and more clearly that we are off-track, then life just takes over. Usually in a way that we don't like at all. We might do our best to avoid it but eventually we are forced to the edge of the abyss, and sometimes even beyond. Life forces us to jump – but only so that we can trust that we will land safely at the bottom. It leads us to exactly those circumstances in which we are most able to grow.

All of us realize in one way or the other when something is changing in our life, when something we wanted isn't bringing us the fulfilment we hoped for. Then it is time to do our homework and to learn something new. This means we have to stop and take a brave and honest look at our life. In most cases, the only way is to seek honest and uncompromising communication with other people. We have to be willing to open up our heart and really follow through on our feelings. If we avoid this, if we repress our inner impulses and our pain or distract ourselves by keeping busy, then often something else happens that sets this process of reorganization in motion. A fateful event, a problem, an illness or the people close to us can all propel us – sometimes against our will – towards self-development.

This path is often much more painful than the responsible way that we avoided earlier. My friend, for example, was later overcome by her own truth in a way that resembled the biblical Deluge rather than a simple flood. She had sensed that things couldn't go on the way they were, that her marriage was empty, that her soul and that of her husband had both been buried under concrete. But she had been afraid to confront her husband. Instead of challenging him with her truth, with all her fears and doubts, she decided to have another baby. Then, in the last term of her pregnancy her husband told her that he was leaving her for another woman.

Truth heals

Even though at the moment everything may seem hopeless to you, even though there may be no solution in sight, be brave and look at your life honestly. Face up to the reality of your situation. The reality is that your relationship probably does not match your dreams. The reality is that your partner doesn't have a clue about how you are feeling. The reality is that you aren't in love any more. The reality is that you know that your partner has distasteful and hurtful qualities. The reality is that you feel jealous or dependent. The reality is that sometimes you would like to get rid of your partner. The reality is that you despise them. The reality is that you have cheated on your partner several times. The reality is that your partner might have cheated on you too. The reality is that you probably got together with your partner for all the wrong reasons.

The reality is that all this is normal in the course of a relationship and presents us with enormous opportunities for healing, as long as we consider our relationship as a place for such healing. The reality is that facing the truth takes courage and continuous work. But often we don't want to bother with that kind of work. We would rather cling to an idealized image of ourselves and our relationship. We would rather go to the Jones's for dinner and invite the Roberts's for tea. We would rather play tennis or collect garden gnomes, go bowling or play golf. We would rather leave our unconscious fears alone. We avoid the work on our deeper feelings because of the risk of even less pleasant sensations turning up.

Of course, relationships are there to provide us with happiness, joy, sensual pleasure and love. Whenever we are not experiencing this state of bliss, they are supposed to heal us so we can experience it again. Whenever a relationship brings us pain, whenever we feel low or unfulfilled, we can use those unpleasant situations as an opportunity for healing.

Another few words of wisdom by Chuck Spezzano:

Find your strength through the gate of weakness.
Find lust and pleasure through the gate of your pain.
Find safety and protection through the gate of your
fears. Find your ability for fulfilment, love and
mutuality through the gate of your loneliness. Find
real and true hope through the gate of your
hopelessness. Find fulfilment through the gate of
what was lacking in your childhood.

11

The adventure of everyday life

We all constantly yearn for adventure, romance and passion. But how is that supposed to happen after 10 or 20 years of marriage? OK, after reading 200 pages or so of this book maybe you are beginning to think that a new lover won't offer much chance of fulfilment either. Maybe you have already been through a divorce and are lapsing into the sobering feeling of familiar gloom. Maybe the last chapter has motivated you to say to yourself: 'Exactly! I am ready for honesty... Well, *some...*'

If you really start to live with honesty and courage, you have no idea how exciting your everyday life can be! We normally adapt to circumstances, we smile nicely, we strive to be exemplary carers, we struggle for recognition and present our jobs and home life as monumentally important. At the same time we dream of strange lands, of freedom, excitement and adventure. The more structured our everyday life, the heavier the chains of our habits, the stronger our desire to escape. We might push it aside and focus on becoming even more exemplary, more dutiful, more consumerist and moving smoothly on up the social ladder – until one day fate catches up with us in the form of a bankruptcy, an illness, a loss, a separation, the discovery of an affair. And all of a sudden floods sweep away everything that was dear to us, everything that was habitual and frozen, everything that followed our rules. They sweep away our reputation, our trust, our feeling of safety, our life of lies, leaving us high and dry. Our life has become more exciting at last, but also more frightening, threatening and unpredictable.

Instead of waiting for this to happen, you could create a few adventures yourself! Stop dreaming your life away. I suggest that you live it fully. Stop running away from everything. Accept what is happening inside yourself. Listen to yourself, check yourself out – and then express yourself. Does this sound like anarchy and chaos to you? It isn't really... If your only means of expression is shouting when you are angry and hurting your partner with your tantrums, you are only damaging yourself. Arguments like that hardly ever have any useful results and they do destroy relationships. However, nothing is more important than finally recognizing your own anger – and fully experiencing it. That is not about simply shouting very loudly, but about being aware of the explosive charge inside you. Let me emphasize that it is *not* about *holding back* the anger. It is about sensing it accurately and accepting it. That way it can be transformed and used as a driving force to take your life forward.

Let go of your feelings

After the first few sessions, clients often ask me whether what they are saying is OK. They feel as if they have completely lost control. Once a person seeks contact with themselves after a long time of inner paralysis, tears will begin to flow where none have flowed before. Surprisingly strong fits of anger will erupt into an otherwise very orderly life. In the beginning this is very good. Very often those feelings have been dammed up for a long time and have to be discharged so that space can be made for a new authenticity. For many people, keeping tight, often unconscious, control over their feelings for years and then releasing them is similar to not doing any exercise for years and then suddenly starting. As long as we don't move much, we don't realize how stiff our muscles are. But after the first training session our whole body feels rusty and stiff. We get out of breath straightaway and our muscles ache for days afterwards.

Once our feelings break out of hiding and into our life, we often develop all sorts of defensive thoughts. As we slowly regain contact with our emotional being we might have to reckon with fear, insecurity and emotional hangovers. But in the same way that our body rewards us with more vitality, agility and beauty after regular training sessions, so our vivacity, our original authenticity and our peace of mind return to us as soon as we give more space to our inner feelings. They are our life energy, our emotional drive. Once we pay attention to them, don't censor them as much, regard them as non-judgementally as possible – basically, if we take them as they come – then we will become whole again. We shouldn't worry when initially feelings flood us like the biblical Deluge. Just imagine a dam breaking – at some point the floods subside and the original river nurtures and fertilizes the parched land again. Your emotions, too, will calm back down to a healthy level.

Together with your feelings, adventure will return to your life – as long as you have the courage to really accept it and to try to understand any seemingly negative messages your emotions may be giving you. Tears are healthy... Anger can liberate... In any case, they are *your* tears, *your* anger, and that is why they are just fine, even if other people dismiss them. Sharing feelings with others is different from aiming them at people. If you simply allow your feelings to resurface, you won't direct them at others. Instead, you will take responsibility for them. You will appear emotional without seeking scapegoats or apportioning blame.

I know a man who is a master of being in touch with his feelings. He loves working with a large audience. But once on the podium he never gives speeches – he *lives* his words. Sometimes he is so touched by what he is saying that tears roll down his cheeks. The next moment he might be laughing heartily, and the whole audience will laugh with him. His words always match exactly what he's feeling. He constantly challenges himself to do exactly what he is telling his audience so passionately to do: to dedicate themselves wholly, to give themselves to life.

I once saw him with his children. He had been parachuting with them, even though he has a terrible fear of heights. He had actually fought this because his children had desperately wanted to try out the parachuting. Of course, they could have done it without him, but he knew enough about the dynamics of families to lead the way as the head of the family. Children have a kind of inner brake system for growth. On a deep level they don't allow themselves to develop further than their parents. That way they keep the order and the closeness within their families. Later, when they want to grow beyond their parents, they very often feel hindered, unconsciously boycott their success or taint their achievements with guilt. This man had decided to grow with his children – and this attitude had brought him an adventure.

Don't take a lover – say what you are thinking instead

Once we find the courage to transcend ourselves and to give ourselves wholly, our life can become exciting, our day-to-day existence can turn into an adventure and our relationships can become fresh and fulfilling again. Giving ourselves wholly means that we are truly expressing ourselves. We are exactly the way we are feeling at any given moment. We are living out our innermost selves, we are ourselves, we are authentic.

Most of all, we are telling each other everything we have kept silent about for years, everything we have repressed or anxiously held back. The only way towards true healing is communication. Separation or divorce means cutting off communication. Most people who separate are unable to talk to each other any more. Either they are afraid of being judged by the other person because of what they might say, or they block all conversations with resentment and bitterness, thereby using the lack of communication as an instrument of power.

But according to statistics, even quite normal couples don't talk to each other for more than ten minutes a day. In contrast to the 1970s and 1980s, according to trend analysts, it is no longer regarded as the 'done thing' to discuss relationships at length. We are living in times of the txt msg. SMS and secret mailboxes preside over marriages and divorces. A short beep can cause a major adrenaline rush – for people in love. It can also cause a panic attack – for suspicious partners. But open and honest discussion that two people not only take part in rationally but actually undertake with all their heart...?

Many couples over the years engage in a communication pattern in which one talks constantly and the other doesn't listen at all. That is as if a river is flowing towards a dam. The emotions are dammed up and build up ... and up ... and at some point the people involved are either numb or they escape the relationship in one way or the other so that their river can flow freely again.

Don't you know what to talk about? All those everyday details which can seem banal are actually very important. Your wife doesn't even know the name of your most important business partner. Your husband doesn't know that last night you had a nightmare about him. Talk about it. Include all the feelings that matter for you. The most important question in everyday communication is: 'How do I want my partner to treat me?' The reason this is so important is because it tells you exactly how you should treat your partner. Most of all, the answer shows you the next step towards healing and re-establishing communication.

You have no idea how exciting your life will be once you truly stand up for yourself, either again or for the first time. What do you think would happen if you finally let it all out? If you stopped being friendly and well-adapted and finally said what you really thought? If you stopped smiling as if your lips were being forced apart? If you stopped pleasing everybody by telling all those little white lies? If at the next dinner party you didn't make small talk about the weather with the person next to you? If you plucked up all your courage and told your partner what you didn't like when making love? If you stopped trying to get things right for your partner just to keep the peace? Your life would turn into an adventure... It would be like waking up. Some fears might arise from the darkness of your unconscious, some emotions might wash over you and your loved ones and rip them from their familiar routines – but you would feel alive.

The biggest adventures in everyday life happen in quiet times. Right now you probably work from dawn till dusk. You strive and struggle and you have lots of hobbies, but there is no time for true leisure. How much excitement do you think would enter your life if you were to grant yourself some peace and solitude? If you were to begin to focus on sensuality, depth, silence and joy?

At first you might feel like an addict in withdrawal – forced to fall back on yourself without any distractions. This encounter with yourself can be quite unsettling. You might become aware for the first time that nothing but your own inner restlessness has made your life so driven and stressful. You might be overpowered by your fears of being abandoned, or of not earning or achieving enough. If you manage to stay with yourself in such a moment, to search for this stillness and to tolerate it, something inside you will slowly stabilize. When you are next in a critical situation, you will feel much less stressed and defensive. You will realize you don't have to be constantly striving for things and you don't always have to be the best.

This process is primarily about sharing our feelings with ourselves and others and just being ourselves. If we are sad, well then, we are sad. And if we are happy, we are happy. Feelings don't last. They are changing all the time. We can't cling on to them and we don't have to repress them either. Our goal is to be in contact with ourselves all the time, to know and to express what is going on for us, without shame and without judgement. It is equally important to keep the same kind of contact with life itself and to accept whatever it presents us with. Even when it is painful to search for the meaning in it.

The present moment is all there is

Life is always about the present moment. If you truthfully admit to yourself that things are not as you'd like them to be, and, furthermore, if you are willing to accept these imperfections, together with all the unwanted feelings, and to let go of resentment and to forgive old hurts, then something very strange will happen: you will arrive – in the middle of your life, in this very moment – at yourself. And in that place there aren't any problems. There is peace.

Nothing I have written in this book is more challenging than this. In order to arrive at this point we have to leave behind our analytical mind. It's not easy to understand that now, at this very moment, everything is OK, even when we have been betrayed, rejected and hurt. We can only be reminded of this deep truth – *re*-minded in a sense. You can only experience this inside yourself. You cannot make it happen. You can only open yourself to it.

There are two areas in our everyday life where we are able to experience this truth: while playing with our children and making love. We all want to be good parents and good lovers. If we are really honest we will know that these are two of the most difficult things to do. Interestingly enough, it is because making love and playing with our children are not about achievement, they are about being. Whenever we try to 'achieve' pleasure we will not get it. How often do we feel helpless and inhibited with our children when they simply want a rough and tumble with us? How often are we haunted by shame and inhibition when we try to be good lovers?

Lust and play have no goals. But nowhere can you find more pleasure, fun, depth and closeness. I once involuntarily said to a client, 'If you want to know what kind of a lover you are in a stable and close relationship then look at the way you play with your children.' If we want to be the kind parents we dream of being, and if we really want to experience lust and fulfilment, then we have to learn to live in the moment.

We are always seeking something. Something is always missing. Maybe you think I'm exaggerating and that you really are quite content. But somehow, everything is about progress, development, achievement. 'That is part of the plan,' you might say... Yes, I agree. Development and evolution are the dynamics of humankind. The problem is the *desire* to achieve. It leads us away from the moment, from everyday life with its countless adventure playgrounds. Who really wants to take life easy? Who accepts that they have just been deceived or have just lost their job? Who will search for the goodness, the opportunity for further development, that life has hidden in this apparent crisis? Who is prepared to be carried away by the river? We are all doggy-paddling – either because we aren't happy with the course of the river or the speed of its flow.

Today I know that absolutely every problem and every obstacle in my life has been a blessing. I also know how long it took me to understand this. I know how much energy it took me to go against the flow of life or to demand something different from what it was presenting to me. If we are not happy with something, we immediately want something different. We feel this inner pull of fear or need and immediately start hunting for success, physical pleasure and approval. And we constantly hope and plead that something will give us happiness or will take away our feelings of fear and need. But whatever we try, our satisfaction is always short-lived. We always want more. Most of the time we are taking part in a race against ourselves that can never be won. 'If only I do this or that or change this or that, then...' But hardly have we reached the 'then' than we tell ourselves, 'Now, if only I do this or change that, then...'

In our mind we are constantly in the future, never in the present. But the possibility of happiness only exists in the now, in the present moment. Only now can I decide to be exactly the way I am – and to accept it with all my heart. Only now can I let go of everything and feel all the goodness in me, no matter what is happening in my life right now.

Our mind constantly suggests to us that we cannot have happiness in the here and now. That it can only be found in an imaginary future. That something has to happen first. That it will take time because we have to understand, learn, clarify, complete, find or solve something or we have to be or have something in order to finally be happy, content and fulfilled. The truth is that none of these brings us closer to happiness. But the feeling is already inside us right now, in the present moment. All that keeps us from it is our ideas about how things *ought* to be.

A life in faith

For that reason we should practise, day in, day out, tracking down all our judgements, expectations and imaginings like a detective. Once we learn to uncover them, there is still the problem of how to let go of them or at least be at ease with them. The most important principle is: everything might not be the way it should be – but it makes sense! I have shown in this book that not everything in my life has been the way I thought it should be. But in hindsight, as I said before, things have always made sense – a higher sense.

Day in, day out, we go round like a hamster in a wheel. We want something, and we want it now. With very important or difficult things we tend to be particularly driven. Then we lose our sense of self and the larger context of which we are a part. Instead of allowing ourselves to be carried onwards, we go on and on, round and round, until one day we can't go on any more. Only then are we forced to confront the heart of the matter. Only then do we have to be still and become aware of ourselves.

Once we have faith in this process, we often learn to simply leap the tracks and stop struggling in order to create some space for a solution. As long as we are struggling, we cannot be aware of what's really happening. But in order to really receive some help, we have to open up. Only then can life take charge again and revert to its natural order.

The next difficult task is already waiting for us: awareness. The question is no longer what you do but what your attitude towards it is. We do most things in life in a kind of inner absence. We read the papers while having breakfast. In the car we think of work. During work we smoke or eat. We are not really present.

And how can we feel good when we are not really present? How can we know what we really need? Once trust is part of our life again, self-awareness and intuition can take their rightful place too. We sense what our body needs and supply it. When working we follow our vocation. We ask ourselves, 'Do I enjoy it? Is it meaningful? Does it help me and others to grow?' We become increasingly aware and present and follow our path, even if it sometimes resembles a rollercoaster, in the firm belief that everything makes sense. Because God is not a person, God is an attitude. A life in faith is a life that allows a situation to change because *we* are changing. Even if it is a miracle.

When people slowly open up to living in the moment and are ready to hold on to their faith even in difficult situations, they neither live in chaos nor spend their time daydreaming. They are not egomaniacs either. They have clear goals without claiming to know every step of the way. While they have the growing courage to express themselves more and more truthfully, they also become more generous towards others. It is a simple principle: if you give yourself wholly, you can take others the way they are too. You don't necessarily get more from others, but you receive more because you are open to it.

With faith, your life will become calmer without you having to make any external changes. It is your attitude that will change. In time, there won't be much that is more important to you than your relationship – but not because you are expecting fulfilment from someone else. Once you are on this path, your relationship will become more and more important because it is the most exciting area in which you can experiment and discover yourself, and because in it you can reveal yourself completely to another human being. The more honesty you have courage for, the more you trust that your partner is the best adventure there is, the more you will sense your own love. And it is some of our rather extravagantly strange partners that offer us the best invitations to deepen our love.

Once we learn to love that way, our life gains a completely new quality. We know that people and relationships are changing all the time. We can truly enjoy the variety that our life and the people around us have to offer. When we live like that, we live from the heart and we give from the heart. To live wholly from the heart means to live fully from the heart. But how can our heart be full when it is no longer filled by the world and everything in it, all the people and all our partners? Because our true source of love is not somewhere out there but is our inner, inexhaustible, divine core.

Can you do the splits? Probably not. If you can, then you are probably challenging your body every day. Most likely you don't have a clue how far your body can be stretched. And my guess is that you probably don't have the faintest idea how far your heart can be opened up. My marriage today has nothing to do with my marriage 10 years ago. But I am certain that as yet I don't have more than a glimpse of what is possible between my husband and me if we stay on this path.

I once met a successful man. He came in, sat down and asked me, 'Why don't my wife, three children and successful career make me happy? What's wrong with me?' He told me that he was woken each night by terrible dreams and had lost all appetite for life. He only had one thought – of running away, of escape. A short time after this confession he was in court, and his fortune and the reputation of his company were at stake. We never found a satisfactory answer to his question and he left my office haunted by thoughts of revenge and by panic attacks. I later heard that he had lost all his money.

Nearly a year later he was back. His body looked rounder, his features softer. As abruptly as before he declared, 'I've sussed it out now. I've always been afraid of life. Last year I learned that life was not out to get me. It loves me. It loves us all, just as we are. It gives us the lessons we need – no matter how difficult they may be. Life is really much wiser than we ever imagine. Once we start to understand life, we discover that it only ever wants one thing from us: for us to grow and find real peace.'

When he told me this, he had lost nearly everything that he had achieved in his life and he didn't know what he was going to do next. But he was closer to his family now than he could ever have imagined.

12

Forgive — you can't change anyone else anyway

Forgiveness – the word itself seems old-fashioned, a remnant of days gone by. But, apart from truthfulness, there is nothing that will transform your life more drastically and heal your relationship more profoundly than forgiveness.

However, forgiveness in this context means something different from what people generally understand by it. Forgiving in our success-orientated society has the flavour of patronizing, of sacrifice, or high morals. In my view, however, it is a powerful healing force, if not the greatest of all healing forces.

As power struggles, beliefs and pain are part of every relationship, no real change is possible without forgiveness. All the hurts that have been accumulating between you and your partner have been building up in your heart and your body like a huge dam that now separates you from each other. For this reason, forgiveness is not a moral concept. It has nothing to do with being generous or having high morals. True forgiveness liberates. It has the effect of a major clearing-out in your heart. True forgiveness is a very radical way of dealing with life. Like most of the other things I have described as truly helpful, forgiveness also demands a change in perspective from the outside to the inside.

To illustrate this, take some time for a little experiment. In your mind, bring up a situation in which you have been hurt. Maybe someone has not looked after you properly, has cheated on you, betrayed or left you. Let the memory of your feelings come up and immerse yourself in this painful story. What images and feelings turn up? Who was it who hurt you? What kind of a situation was it? Do you feel resentment, anger, helplessness or fear? Do you feel a tension in your body? Is your stomach or chest tightening up, your throat constricting? Are your shoulders tense? Do you feel numb? Angry? All churned up?

Take some time to really experience those feelings. Whatever is happening in you when you are remembering this old hurt, it is happening within *you*. Allow yourself to remain aware of this. Dare to observe what is happening inside you the way a sport reporter watches the players on the pitch. All those memories, all the helplessness, the paralysis, the anger, are inside you. Not with the person who hurt you, not somewhere out there. Right now nothing has happened other than me asking you a few questions. It is *your* thoughts, *your* images, *your* emotions, *your* physical tension. *You* are feeling bad when you are thinking of an old hurt. *You* are feeling bad because you still feel the hurt.

I am sure there have been all sorts of unpleasant things between you and your partner. Maybe it has been really painful. Maybe at some point the pain has seemed unbearable. Maybe you have felt numerous little stabs to your heart. If we are hurt by something, it is important to admit to that, to allow the rising anger. But what good does it do to do this time and again? It is we, after all, who keep hurting, it is we who are robbed of all power and confidence, because we remain chained to people and events from the past.

Resentment makes you ill

Most people seem to take an almost masochistic pleasure in ruminating on old pain, in digging up all the memories, all the hurts, all the helplessness or the anger. But if you do this, it stays with you. None of those feelings are with the person who has hurt you. Nothing of it can be found outside you. It is *your* thoughts regarding this person, this situation. *You* are feeling bad. The other person isn't even present. They aren't shouting at you, leaving you, cheating on you. You are only thinking of something they have done and could do again. And you feel bad almost immediately.

'Of course!' I hear you say. 'It's only natural. Of course I'm hurt. After all, my partner cheated on me, never really cared for the children and humiliated me.' You think that in the light of all that you are entitled to be resentful. Maybe you *are* entitled. But do you really enjoy it? Maybe this question sounds absurd. Does anyone really enjoy feeling bad? But nobody has ever encouraged us to ask this question in terms of our response to emotional pain. Forgiveness mainly means valuing your own inner peace more than the urge to repeatedly subject yourself and others to old patterns and demands. When we forgive, we are free. Forgiveness is like a solvent that gets rid of the guilt, resentment, self-hatred and judgements sticking to us.

A recent American study on the effects of forgiveness for emotional pain came to the conclusion that forgiveness is good for body and soul. It found that continuous resentment makes you ill and prevents new and healthy developments. Forgiving is good for you – it brings about new ways of living.

Nearly 260 participants were invited by psychologists under Dr Frederic Luskin from Stanford University to a 90-minute session during which they could practise forgiveness. They were encouraged to talk about emotional hurts they had suffered. They could listen to lectures on forgiveness or enter into an inner dialogue with the people who had offended or humiliated them. At the end of the project, the majority of the participants said they felt less pain than before. Psychological and physical stress symptoms such as back pain, insomnia or stomach complaints occurred less frequently. The leader of the study, Dr Frederic Luskin, described forgiveness as the beginning and the end of a healing process. People who can't forgive waste their energy on anger, desire for revenge, hatred, bitterness and wrath. Forgiveness, however, offers the chance to let fall the chains of the past.

Maybe you have been inspired by the results of this study to look at forgiveness from a new viewpoint: practising forgiveness is our right not to be tortured by the past any more. To remain stuck in anger and scapegoating robs us of the possibility of mourning our hurts and moving on. If we don't acknowledge our pain and process it, and instead stay stuck with anger, bitterness and resentment, then the pain not only stays within us, it becomes rigid and paralyzes and burdens us.

The most important cleansing task is to mourn. It is important for us to mourn painful events appropriately. Only then can we get over the pain, let go of it and begin something new. No pain can truly be healed if it has not been acknowledged, grieved and forgiven.

Forgiving others means freeing yourself

But there is a nasty trap hidden on this path. Don't cut yourself off heroically from all your old hurts by expecting yourself to practise generosity and understanding with all kinds of behaviour. If pain is repressed too much, it causes a kind of inner poisoning – grief that is not expressed often leads to depression. To smile and patronizingly indulge the bad behaviour of others, to excuse everything and even deny our pain has nothing to do with forgiveness. Forgiveness is more concerned with a radical change of position: 'I don't want to be the victim any more and I don't want to feel bad about myself. That is why I am letting go of the past now and concentrating on myself and my own way forward.' When you can do this, you can stop clinging to the old pain and reconcile yourself to the way things were. This kind of forgiveness is not easy in the beginning – but it heals. Most importantly, it's something you do for yourself.

Once we recognize that our unpleasant feelings are not part of the other person and not their responsibility, we have come a long way. Even if it is quite obvious that the other person bears some of the guilt, the feelings, the response to what happened, are ours, and they may have been for a long time. Often one incident only adds to a pile of unprocessed pain on the same subject. That has all simply been waiting for a trigger in order to rise to the surface of our consciousness again. That is part of our evolution – a mechanism that life has organized brilliantly: all our pain, all our hurts and all our beliefs at some point turn up in order to be healed. All conflicts, accidents and attacks only mirror what is on our mind, and they are all the result of our own thoughts, beliefs and impulses.

This doesn't mean taking on blame and guilt for another person. Everything that happens to us only shows us the depth of our own pain. If we accept this connection between outer and inner, guilt doesn't arise. Instead we finally gain insight, strength and the responsibility to perceive ourselves as whole.

Regarding our relationships with other people, only one thing is really important: we have to track down the negativity in our own mind and look at it. The stigma that we have attached to ourselves is always the most difficult to see. But only we decide what hurts us, what we deem negative and associate with unpleasant feelings. For that reason we need to recognize how we create our own personal suffering by clinging on to negative beliefs about other people and events. If you don't recognize how you are doing this time and again, then you will carry on doing it time and again. And you will fail to understand why your life is so difficult. You will make others and their 'otherness' responsible for your own problems – usually your partner, but also your parents, your children, your boss, your neighbours or society in general.

Parents are like dumbbells

Resentment, blaming, judgements and beliefs are the poison of life. Every negative judgement about another person is a hidden attack on the self. That is why our mind needs regular training to detox our entrenched ways of thinking and judging. Your best sparring partners in this are your parents. I love the following statement regarding our parents: parents are not here to get everything right for us, to continuously support us and to nurture us; parents are rather like dumbbells, used to counterbalance our life and to strengthen the muscles of our soul. Whenever you are quarrelling with your roots, try to see it from this point of view. Ask yourself what strength you could develop or have already developed because of the inadequacies of your parents. Eventually you might even be able to thank your parents for it.

In other cultures such a process is part of life. Native Americans, for example, honoured particular tribe members as 'anti-humans'. They had to do the opposite of what everybody else did to remind the tribe that all concepts of 'right' and 'wrong' were relative. In the Sufi tradition there is a spiritual discipline called the 'path of reproach' reminding the followers to justify the questionable actions of others as far as possible. Once on this path, you even can be inspired to seek out those you don't like. In India, meanwhile, the principle of non-violence is based on the acceptance of the innate imperfection of man. According to Gandhi, the enemy is both without and within, and we have to strive for the reconciliation of those two manifestations of it.

If we don't practise this kind of openness towards others we turn into victims of our own superhuman demands on ourselves. Deep inside we have beliefs like 'I'm not allowed to make mistakes. I always have to be perfect and present myself as such, otherwise people will think I am a failure. I'm not good enough – that's why I need others to accept me. If they reject me, I am no good.'

If we learn to accept that we are not perfect and allow ourselves to make mistakes, then we can also stop expecting other people to be perfect. The less we strive for perfection ourselves, the more we defuse our judgements and assessments of others.

Jenny is always afraid that people might talk about her. She's always asking you not to talk about this and that, saying that it's confidential and nobody is to know about it. Whenever she meets people she has to keep it a secret because she also knows other people's secrets. Jenny is a first-class secret-keeper and always wary of spies and gossipmongers. When talking to her, though, it is very difficult not to judge others. Nothing escapes Jenny's critical and sometimes ruthless assessment. She approaches everything with both doubts and firm beliefs. She has hardly ever forgiven anything. If Jenny could look at herself from the outside, she would condemn herself as a merciless gossipmonger. If she could really see herself, she would recognize all her fears, insecurities and perfectionist traits. If Jenny could open her heart to herself, she would feel her longing for closeness and her desire for real and open encounters with others.

First and foremost forgiveness is important for *us* in terms of our self-rejection, our demands, our standards and our perfectionism. If we don't know yet what we want to forgive, then forgiveness, like everything else, needs willingness followed by practice and commitment. Look at your partner, your parents, your bosses and colleagues, your friends and relatives and *practise*, in the true sense of the word, forgiveness. If you catch yourself gossiping about them again, judging them and getting upset about their behaviour, then remind yourself that you have just learned something about your own ruthlessness towards yourself. Remember your own desire for closeness, your shame, the ways in which you compensate for your own insecurity. Practise compassion, understanding and gentleness or simply let go of the whole thing. You probably won't manage this in a day, but whenever you catch yourself judging something or someone, the more you practise letting go, the more peaceful your life and your relationships will become.

If you want to find out whether you have practised enough, just listen to your inner self. You will immediately recognize true forgiveness. Something inside you loosens up, tension decreases. Your feelings calm down. Your way of looking at that person or situation has changed. You feel at ease – freer, lighter and more flexible. New things are possible.

True miracles

Sometimes we dream of a miracle happening to our relationship, but the only real miracle is forgiveness. But each minute offers us the opportunity to decide whether to let this miracle happen. Every moment that passes, we can decide whether we want to feel resentful or whether we want to finally let go of the past. It is in our hands whether we feel slimy frog's skin or the magically transformed heart of a prince in need of liberation. At any moment we can choose to let go of our old pain. The miracle is a simple change of perspective, the opening up of a new panorama. And we don't have to make this miracle happen – we can simply ask for it.

It is probably not an everyday habit of yours to simply ask for a miracle when things go off the rails. We have learned to look for scapegoats, to become defensive and to judge other people, especially in difficult situations, but never to simply turn inward and pray for help.

When a situation overwhelms you and you find yourself making judgements, if you find that you cannot make peace with the other person on your own, if you cannot look at things in a different way, then ask for a miracle. All you need is willingness to forgive – even if you don't feel able to do it yet. Just admit to yourself that right now you don't have the strength to leave all the condemnation and resentment behind. Acknowledge the resentment that prevents you from choosing to embrace love and forgiveness. Simply prepare to *want* to forgive. Prepare for belief in the underlying divine connection and the immeasurable availability of help. Even when you still feel bitter, when your heart can't find peace, you can experience true miracles. You only have to ask for them. Your willingness to forgive will summon all the help in the universe, because 'The holiest of all places is where old hatred is turned to love.'[2]

2. *A Course in Miracles*, The Foundation for Inner Peace, Arkana, 1997

13

Love and lust

Just in case you don't quite know what this chapter is about while reading the next few lines, let me announce it clearly right here: this chapter is about sexuality – or rather it's about physical love.

This morning I woke up and everything I felt and saw was saturated by love. I know how corny that might sound. But it is the truth. I could now easily continue in the vein of a romantic love song and describe the feelings that flooded me like gentle waves all morning. The transition from night to day was a soft one and I found myself still in the same lovely sensual oceanic state. I stayed in bed with my eyes closed and enjoyed surfing through my body. Soft warm waves tickled me everywhere and gave me a feeling of being utterly alive, of being capable of anything. Opening my eyes wasn't easy, but the world out there also seemed rich and abundant. The colours of the autumn leaves in our garden seemed stronger and more vibrant than before. When I jogged through the woods, the earthy smell was richer and more intense. At some point I stopped running so that I could experience every single step on the soft earth more intensely. Time and again a thought went through my head: 'Everything is possible!'

Everything is possible

Do you want to know the reason for this divine state of mine? After two tough days of tension, overshadowed by the past, my husband and I met again last night in a deep and heartfelt way and made love. The important word here is 'love'. Even more importantly, I am not talking about sex here, but about physical *love*. We had both loved, through our pain and our sullenness, until we could find our true and peaceful nature in each other again. We had stayed together until finally our hearts and bodies could fill up again with love and join each other until the nourishing stream between us was flowing freely again.

We both know that we love each other deeply and with all our heart. We both know by now that our relationship has really gone beyond such days of tension and conflict. During those two days it was as if we were both suffering from hallucinations, as if we were seeing each other as monsters, as if we were hearing malicious voices. In reality we know that no one is responsible for our own negative feelings. We know that we only slide into that state when we have not looked after ourselves well enough, when things are too hectic or when we are under pressure to meet external demands. We know that we become obnoxious and sterile if we don't take the time to let go and play. We know what will happen if we tick off jobs like robots and don't take the time to see each other's heart, if we work mechanically through lists and don't ask each other how we really feel. We have known for a long time that we lose contact with ourselves that way and lose contact with love as well. We know that a clash is inevitable then. And still it happens to us – though not as often as it used to.

By now my husband and I are quite experienced in muddling through the occasional dip and crossing the next relationship ditch, hopefully without injury. This time we argued more and more frequently about increasingly trivial issues for two days. My husband repeatedly tried to escape and I just pursued him the whole time. Little things made us go for each other like two terriers. Whenever I managed to relax for a moment in between bouts I tried to explore as thoroughly as possible what it was that was pushing its way up to the surface, what old pain it was that was crying out to be healed. Then I realized that the first crack had opened when we had been in a particularly good mood and had decided to go dancing. We hadn't danced for a long time. But on the dance floor our bodies only moved mechanically, routinely, habitually, without any real contact. While my husband eventually started looking around vaguely, I tried to catch his eye and became tense. We carried on dancing, but it was as if we were immune to each other. We touched, but not really. Worst of all, we didn't address this feeling but simply tried to ignore it.

It was that night that the nagging and the tension between us started. Finally, after yet another argumentative and unpleasant day, we managed to find words for what was happening. Slowly, bit by bit, we began to express what we were feeling and what we were really missing. It turned out that behind all that niggling we both had felt insecure, rejected and a failure when out dancing – but neither of us had been conscious of it in the slightest.

Our conversation was a bit like a cotton bud with iodine on it being placed over an open wound. It was necessary for clearing the mind and cleansing the soul, but what remained was a stinging pain. One wrong word and my husband froze. One more defensive retreat and my nagging and pestering continued. We were back with our old issues, trawling through all our old emotional baggage. But as we are now very experienced at this, we also looked for our love in between. That night we went to bed with the firm intention of retrieving our openness, our peace of mind and our mutual contact before the day was out. We didn't want to take all that pain and anger through the night. So there was no other way but to express everything that was between us, because only that way would we ever find our love again.

The river of love

We went to bed, face to face, and looked each other in the eye – not without resistance at first, but we knew this would be a good way to be honest. Calm was restored and we were able to make the effort to talk to each other again straight from the heart, to slowly begin touching each other again with love until our bodies were filled again with a peaceful vitality. At first we only touched each other in a wary and alert way, as if picking our way through a field of landmines. But then something happened which you cannot make happen, you simply have to let happen: something within us began to relax and our bodies found their way back to their own peaceful, powerful flow. Never before had I been able to perceive so clearly and consciously that as I saw myself more and more clearly and shared my pain, everything inside me filled up with life again. It was as if my whole body had been blocked. And slowly I began to feel love again. My love could flow more freely through me and it had only one goal – to reconnect with my husband.

I have written every single word of the last few paragraphs as a passionate plea to illustrate that there is deep innocence inside our bodies and our sexuality waiting to be accepted, to be freed from shame and to be acquitted. Nothing has been raped more violently than physical love. Sexuality has been distorted as pornography, pursued and driven to excess, condemned and shamed by the churches, and in countless bedrooms it has simply dried out and died.

Consciously or unconsciously, everybody longs for their life to be nurtured and enriched by physical love, but hardly anybody knows the ancient secrets of sexual energy that give us sparkle, connectedness and peace in mind and body. Most people struggle through puberty in search of satisfying and bonding physical love. Most of them find themselves either with a broken heart or in a sexual dead-end street. Only a few find the key that can open the door to fulfilling sexuality for good.

I remember the uneasy feeling after I had slept with a boy for the first time. I had been lucky really. My first boyfriend was a wonderfully sensitive person whom I trusted. But still, after our first night I felt strangely empty and disappointed. Was that all? Was that what everybody dreamed and talked about incessantly – at school or at home behind closed doors?

Searching for the secrets of physical love

After that I started looking for something I didn't have a clue about. I was curious, uninhibited and open, and had all kinds of sexual experiences. Sometimes it was surprising, as if I had discovered something important. Often it was fun or exciting, sometimes I was even insatiable, wild or entranced. But on the whole there was always something missing and I never felt deeply touched for long. My heart was still yearning and more and more often I felt a kind of lingering sadness. I would split up with one man, only sooner or later to end up in the arms of another, and it seemed as if the greatest secret of life kept escaping me. The crazy thing was that I had never experienced it but something inside me knew that there was a secret. So I kept on searching...

There were situations and events in my life that at first, and even second, glance didn't seem to have anything to do with sex, but they were totally different from anything else I had ever experienced. At times, for a brief moment, I felt fulfilled. Space and time seemed to disappear and I felt free of everything, full of love and deeply connected. It was as if all burdens had fallen from me and, as if led by a magical power, I had glimpsed my own being. Back then I had no words to describe this boundless and unreal sense of happiness. I was worried that an attempt to describe it would sound crazy and so I didn't dare to share my feelings with others. That's why I never had any idea that sexuality could have something to do with the feeling or that the feeling could have something to do with sexuality.

Later I discovered that the feeling only happened when I was unusually relaxed. I noticed with surprise that it occurred several times when I couldn't control events, had challenged myself beyond my limits and was determined to control something that was evading me. It was years before I read something about sex that made the connection, something that has stayed with me ever since. I was married to my husband by then and already had the feeling that sex with him would not bring me what my inner being was longing for so much. That's when I came across a book by the Australian writer Barry Long with the title *Making Love: Sexual Love the Divine Way*. His central thesis was that whenever a woman felt that her man was driven by a sexual urge and not by nurturing love, she should say no.

The womb gives birth to all things

A book on sex that was out to ban sex from our bedrooms...?
A book written by a man that started with the following
words:

> *Woman's basic unhappiness, her perennial discontent,*
> *is because man can no longer reach her physically.*
> *Her emotional excess, depressions, tearful*
> *frustrations, even premenstrual tension and the*
> *conditions leading to hysterectomy and other uterine*
> *problems, are due to man's sexual failure to gather*
> *or release in lovemaking her finest, fundamental,*
> *female energies. These extraordinary beautiful divine*
> *energies are intense and exquisite and when left*
> *untapped in woman, as they are now, they degenerate*
> *into psychic and emotional disturbances, and*
> *eventually crystallize into physical abnormalities. The*
> *womb gives birth to all things.*[3]

To me it sounded like a pamphlet by a hardcore feminist, but
it had been written by a 70-year-old man who loved sex and
loved women. It was a radical challenge to men to abandon
their sex drive in favour of love.

> *To be able to love in this way is the authority man*
> *has lost – his only true authority over woman.*
> *This requires pure love. It does not depend on*
> *technique. A man may develop his sexual technique*
> *but he cannot use expertise to make divine love.*

....
3. Barry Long, *Making Love: Sexual Love the Divine Way*, Barry Long
Books, London, 1998, p.7

Exciting sensations and orgasms are gratifying and give him a form of authority, but they are not the love that woman craves. He may satisfy her, like a good meal. But soon she hungers again and eventually despises her appetite or herself, because she knows she is not being loved.[4]

I had never connected my inner restlessness, my continuous searching, so clearly with sex. For me, Barry Long's words were very radical. But something in my heart whispered: 'Yes, yes!' But I wasn't a feminist! Quite the opposite – women had often accused me of being too understanding towards men. I loved men and respected them. And now male sex was supposed to have polluted women? Long claimed it had even turned us into harpies, bitches, emotional demons:

While the world continues as it is, the fiendess will not allow man to forget his failure to love woman rightly. Woman must be loved. The future of the human race depends on woman being loved because only when woman is truly loved can man be truly himself and regain his lost authority.[5]

In spite of all the radical anti-maleness, I wanted to know what this divine physical love was and how you could experience physical love in a divine way. So I finished Long's little book. It remained radical until the last sentence, but it made more sense to me than anything I had come across before. The more I read, the more I discovered that his words, in spite of their radicalism, were the most reconciling and loving that I

4. Ibid., p.9
5. Ibid., p.10

had ever read about sex for – luckily, as it turned out – both men and women.

Since then as a therapist I have heard many men and women talk about their disappointing sex lives. A while ago I read an interview with an established producer of pornography on growth and trends in the field. The films most successful with male clients were the ones with a contemporary flair. 'At the moment the fashion is not to show horny women but women who refuse to go along with it,' the producer explained coolly.

Today I know that real sexual love can offer a way forward to men and women, away from unwillingness, driven sex, boredom and desperate relationships. I know that this kind of love can change your relationship fundamentally. You have to make a decision, though. You have to decide on a new form of physical love with your old partner – yes, that partner you may have dismissed as not all that interesting. To begin with, it is sufficient to admit that you won't find the sexual fulfilment that you really long for, that you don't really know how to get it. It is enough to simply long to find a better way. It is enough to be prepared to be yourself with your partner – whether this means being helpless, vulnerable, angry, rejecting, starved, bitter or frigid. This may not match any of the ideals of sex, love and relationships that you have ever heard of, read about or imagined. But this radical u-turn is needed for your sexuality and your relationship to truly heal.

Beyond orgasm

Rather than constantly work towards an orgasm, to long for it, to focus and fixate on the climax, just relax into your natural sexual energy. It is frequently buried but always present. Rather than put pressure on yourself to do or be something else, you should be prepared for a kind of emotional withdrawal from your fantasies, images and ideas of brilliant sex. Men as well as women have to practise loving each other without thoughts, goals, emotions and fantasies. Initially this will feel strange, but it leads to abandoning all control and leaving a sexual encounter truly to the bodies and their impulses.

Maybe you are not aware of this, but sexuality is often about control – most of all about control of the self. We control ourselves – continuously, though mostly unconsciously – in order to meet our own demands and standards. We control our sexuality, we play games, we turn ourselves on and stimulate desire – only we don't trust our own natural inner flow and our true being. Women especially need the courage to accept their physical hardening and their emotional starvation. Strictly speaking, they need the courage not to fake another orgasm or to let sex happen just to please their partner. Be brave enough to acknowledge all your fears of failure, your feelings of inferiority and your latent anger at your partner and to express them.

Men need the courage to recognize that they often ejaculate but only rarely experience an orgasm and to become fully aware of their bodies. Men are rarely in real touch with their physicality and should admit to themselves and their partners how little they know or have so far wanted to know about their physical and emotional needs, and how inhibited and insecure they feel.

When you first present yourself in this nakedness you might feel as if someone has deliberately ripped the last little seedlings from your barren field and viciously trampled on them. Maybe in the light of your new-found awareness and open discussion everything appears even bleaker and more hopeless than before. Maybe stepping off the path of your narrow routines or leaving behind the physical silence of the past makes you feel inhibited and shaken. Maybe you feel ashamed and think, 'I can't do this! I'd rather split up with my partner than try something like this!' or 'That'll never work with my partner after all these years!' Maybe you aren't aware of any thoughts like that but simply feel resistant to the idea.

The phantom of passion

If you stay with it, in spite of all this, and muster up all your courage, it can still take months, maybe even years, for you and your partner to wade through the swamp of misunderstandings, hardening fronts, anger and misled fantasies. You might have to acknowledge that your original passion was for a phantom ideal rather than your real partner. You are likely to recognize ever more clearly that your partner is just as vulnerable and imperfect as you are. They might say 'no' or lack imagination – that is simply because they don't know any better.

You will probably find that despite all your desire for satisfying and passionate sex you too are just as cut off from your body most of the time. Throughout the day you may hardly feel anything of its finely tuned impulses. Maybe you treat it with very little sensuality. Maybe your normal life is often hectic and anything but orgiastic. Maybe you often think of sex but rarely feel physically comfortable. You might even just be looking for someone who neglects your body and your soul less than you do.

Admitting to all this might sound alarming, but don't run away from it. Keep going and be determined to feel all your feelings and – most of all – to express them as openly as you can to your partner. In the end you will be able to be the best teachers for each other and to supply the best possible sex for each other. In time, something will grow between you – a new kind of love and trust that maybe you have never experienced in your life before. Unlike the first 'blind' passion, it will be a solid and stable bond that can make true, deep, physical love possible.

Forget about sex

You cannot consciously make this happen or even force it. You can only relax and open yourself to it. The more you learn to trust in your own love, the more it will spread within you. This takes time and patience and means shedding a lot of old habits. I can't emphasize often enough that first and foremost we have to unlearn our fixation on the orgasm. In order to find yourself again in the natural and fulfilling flow of physical love, you have to be willing to consciously touch and explore each other's bodies, even though you might feel cold, weak and numb at first.

Stop waiting for an extraordinary lover, a special mistress, a secret passion or thrilling affair to somehow enter your life! Do it with your partner, even if at first it feels uncomfortable and you would rather run away. Don't give up if you feel like a sexless robot or a driven sex addict. If you don't feel good enough because you haven't felt any desire for your partner for a while, if you find it all too much, if you feel like a racehorse in its box that is not allowed to run, if when you become aware of your body you are overwhelmed by a quickie or a fantasy, if you live with constant desire and expectations but can't share your kinky fantasies with your partner, then you should throw overboard all your expectations, demands and dreams of ideal sex. Forget porn videos, sexy lingerie and alternative practices. Instead, reawaken love within yourself by committing yourself to your real, breathing partner and your equally real and solid body. Decide to completely commit yourself to your partner and above all to yourself. Prepare yourself for an intimate encounter – mostly with your own body.

You will probably be amazed at how little contact you have with your body. It has probably been ages since you have listened to it consciously, felt it and loved it.

Ask your partner to look into your eyes silently. At first this might be very difficult. You might feel embarrassed, or ashamed, or want to laugh. Stay with it anyway and simply let things take their own course. Talk about what is happening within you. Share with each other your physical sensations – the unpleasant ones too. But don't talk about what you are thinking – instead say what you are truly *feeling*. Examine the sensations that arise in your body one by one. If a sensation is pleasant, tell your partner so that they can feel more secure on this new path. If it isn't pleasant, dare to stay with it anyway. Go inside yourself, open up within without severing the contact to your partner. Feel your body and trace what it is telling you. Allow your breathing to become deeper – this will relax you.

Be aware of every single sensation inside you – tension here, a tickling there, maybe nothing particular in other places. Stay alert! Recognize the point at which you shift from simple observations to judgements and values, such as: 'I am feeling this here, but I should be feeling...' 'My partner does this here, but they should really...'

Helplessness, sadness and anger may surface and tear you away from the moment. Maybe excitement and desire will develop just as you begin to relax and will drive you into wanting and pursuing. Don't let yourself be driven by your expectations – acknowledge your arousal, stay in the moment and open up from the lower part of your body into other parts. Focus on your hands and feet and on your chest. The chest is where your heart is, and true physical love always comes from the heart.

True physical love comes from the heart

Only when a woman's heart can make contact with a man's can her body truly open up. Once she can get through to his softness, the insecurity of his being, she can feel herself inside him and real contact can happen. This is the point Barry Long makes in his seemingly anti-male and anti-sex book: true physical love comes from the heart. That is why he strongly condemns the male fixation on genitalia and orgasms, pornography and sexual fantasies.

A man only becomes calm when he has been able to pour his loving strength physically into a woman. A woman who can truly receive opens up her heart and gives energy through her breasts into his heart, from where it can flow back into his genitalia. Only when men and women are linked in their hearts and are open and present with their whole bodies can such a circuit of love be complete. Many people who have experienced this circulation describe it as a kind of all-body orgasm, a feeling of boundlessness and complete unity.

You don't need to be the perfect lover to experience this spiritual dimension of sex. All this is only about one issue: are we prepared to open up to our partner and our old hurts? Are we prepared to cut through old blockages, to feel them, accept them, to share them and to heal?

When my husband and I began this we had a very special experience and I finally grasped what physical love was really all about. He and I had opened up widely to each other and had connected very deeply. He had penetrated me lovingly and then, all of a sudden, I had felt a stabbing pain in my heart. Every time my husband pushed inside me my heart ached more. I was disheartened and surprised – there was an obvious connection between my heart and my lower body. It seemed that there was a wall between them that my husband could not overcome. We talked to each other and stayed close. I shared my tears with him, he his love with me. Later we agreed that it had been a very special encounter that had brought us closer together.

Many women have described to me their pain, fear and numbness and an inexplicable aggressive tension in their body. 'I was standing in the kitchen making dinner,' one woman said, 'when my husband came in and put his arms around my waist. Within seconds my whole body was completely tense and rejecting.' This woman hadn't got a brute for a husband and she felt ashamed telling me this. Frequently women become furious with regard to their breasts. 'I can't bear how he kneads and grabs my breasts.'

For female sexuality to heal it is vital that women trust their perception of touch again and have the courage to express what it means to them. It only takes women a fraction of a second to recognize the purpose of a touch. Is it about sexual desire or about tenderness and love? Women know that instantly. But they only rarely dare to share with their partners how angry and helpless they feel when grabbed in a loveless and greedy way. Far too often they feel at odds with their own bodies and think of themselves as abnormal or frigid when they tense up. Most men, meanwhile, are so starved of female receptiveness and openness that their emotionally undernourished bodies can only respond with hunger. Women, like men, often find these days that their genitals in a sexual encounter feel hard and numb, sometimes even painful or dead. Pain and numbness are symptoms of extreme tension.

Our body is our memory

Our body is our memory – all our past experiences are stored there, in the tissues of our cells. In that sense, every person's sexual history is stored in their body, in all its pleasant and unpleasant aspects. The breasts and vaginas of women often have lots of pain, emotion and tension stored up from the past. Once we connect consciously with our body, once we make love consciously, then our sexual past surfaces so that we can finally heal it and rid our body of it at last.

Once we begin to practise true physical love, once all our movements become slower and more conscious, our genitalia will start healing and both physical and emotional pain from the past will surface. Don't turn away from this pain – acknowledge it as precisely and lovingly as you can and share it with your partner. For some men it is particularly important to give voice to their pain, to express it in words and to let go of it with a moan or a sound from deep inside.

Whenever you feel pain, numbness and tension in your body, look at it from a different angle: be grateful for this feeling because it is showing you exactly where in your body a healing touch is needed.

Once you consciously attend to tension, numbness or actual pain with tenderness and with few words, often very soon something begins to relax in your body or in your feelings.

Sometimes tears begin to flow, sometimes you become furious, sometimes all you want to do is run away, or you feel intense feelings and sensitivity flowing to the parts that were numb before. Sometimes your whole body fills with life and love and you connect instinctively and in fluid movements with your partner. Sometimes you just start laughing. Keep laughing. Your partner might start as well. In sexuality, as in relationships in general, humour is one of the most powerful healing forces – especially when things are really bad. Many people have suffered serious sexual hurt. Humour can heal that deep pain.

Whether you want to laugh or cry, just do it. Meet your partner physically, even if your love life has been dormant or just routine. Give up all your old habits and simply love each other. Lie down together. Don't do anything, just wait, be aware of yourself, acknowledge your body and follow it. Do it as often as you can. The more often you make this effort to open up for love, the more love will grow between you. The less often you practise physical love – no matter how often you are having sex – the more you will drift apart. The more often you connect in physical love, the more healing it is for your relationship.

You will find that sexual harmony is vitally important for contentment in love. Frequent physical connectedness strengthens the emotional bond, creates trust and makes our bodies calmer and more balanced.

Once on this path, we become more cheerful. Sometimes we get high and surf blissfully through a whole day, as I did at the beginning of this chapter. When we connect in physical love more often, we will become more loving and let other people and issues just be. Sex will have a totally different function. It will lose its mythical aspects and become a gateway to love and connection. And we will be free of the pressure of our own expectations.

Do it as often as you can

Don't get me wrong – don't let those last few lines actually put you under pressure. 'Now she's saying that we have to have sex more often!' That is not my point. You don't have to do anything. No positions, no orgasms, no exciting adventures, secret practices or special lust and passion. I'm simply advocating being yourself as often as you can. And connecting as often as you can with your partner. Take the time for a truly intimate encounter. And for that you have to get out of your head and into your body, into the Here and Now.

You might not get any orgiastic feelings at first; instead you might meet numbness, boredom or shame, posturing like bouncers at the door of a glittering nightclub. That's OK. Just stay on this path and love the other person just as they are. And persevere, even during setbacks. You know now that on this journey many a repressed emotion will be set free. Arguments might erupt, emotional outbursts break out. Feelings can fluctuate like a ship in a storm. Ride the waves rather than let yourself be carried away by them. Observe your own emotions and be on the lookout for love. That way it will spread and connect you and your partner more firmly.

Once you try this, you will realize more and more clearly how totally different the flow of physical love is from just having sex. If you stay with it, you may well discover what you have been seeking for years. You will be able to experience true intimacy again and can let your love grow. You can rediscover your sexual energy, your life force and your inner peace. Your body can trust itself again. Old hurts can be addressed and your body can truly relax at last.

I am convinced that physical love is deeply rooted in human nature, that when we open up our heart to someone, it quite automatically flows from us to them. All we have to do is let it happen. For that we need to rediscover our innocence – the feeling that everything is fine, no matter what we feel or don't feel. We don't need anything for our sexuality to return – it isn't about positions, knowledge, skills or frequency. It isn't about desire and lust either. It is about the physical expression of love.

We often hear of miraculous healing taking place when mentally impaired people receive physical attention. Be it people in a deep coma or people with Alzheimer's, they respond positively to a tender loving touch, even though they might barely be able to navigate their way through their own lives any more. I recently read about a home for Alzheimer's patients. Several dozen people lived there, mostly elderly. Most of them were so confused that they didn't recognize their closest relatives any more and could remember only fragments of their former life. The director of the home was convinced that their humanity could flow again freely when freed of all demands of the self, of society and of duty. 'Nearly half of our clients are sexually active,' he said, 'People who need help with feeding and who find thinking difficult begin to fall in love here and to feel desire – with all that that implies. When we have a party in the home, the women's eyes begin to sparkle as if they were 18 again. And the men are tender and full of energy.'

In one of his books, *Eleven Minutes*, the Latin American writer Paulo Coelho tries to discover the secret of sexuality. He asks the remarkable question: 'How can you touch a soul?

By love or by lust?' The protagonist, the prostitute Maria, gives the answer in her diary:

What does this painter want of me? Doesn't he realize that we are from different countries, cultures and sexes? Does he think that I know more about pleasure than he does and wants to learn something from me?

... He's an artist. He should know that the great aim of every human being is to understand the meaning of total love. Love is not to be found in someone else, but in ourselves; we simply awaken it. But in order to do that, we need the other person. The universe only makes sense when we have someone to share our feelings with.

He says he's tired of sex. So am I, and yet neither of us really knows what that means.[6]

6. Paulo Coelho, *Eleven Minutes*, HarperCollins, London, 2004, p.118

14

Children of love

Some relationships break up when the couple remains child-less. Some couples are only together because of the children. Some relationships undergo their first major rift at the birth of the first child... Children have enormous power. Children carry the hope of a family and are its mirror. Children don't need friendliness, they demand real closeness, and so they bring out every inadequacy in their parents and transform every relationship. Children demand utter commitment. With seismographic precision they reflect in their behaviour what their parents really believe, not just what they say, and what the parents' relationship is truly like.

I'd like to venture into the realm of statistics one more time to illustrate a phenomenon which our society is only very vaguely aware of. In third place on the list of reasons for divorce is: 'Changes after the birth of the first child.' When did the problems between you and your partner start? When did you lose your appetite for sex? Since when has your partner been having affairs? When did your marriage lose its sparkle? When did the love disappear? I don't know how often I have had these questions answered by the same sad, guilty look and the words: 'Since our baby was born.'

I don't think there is much awareness in our society of the true impact of childbirth. A friend of mine who had a baby several months ago rang me recently. She said, 'You know, nothing can prepare you for this. You cannot possibly believe it beforehand, let alone understand it. A woman who has given birth has nothing in common with one who hasn't.' My friend had just spent a whole night looking after her feverish baby while suffering from cystitis herself. In the morning she was totally exhausted, but she was amazed at herself, at how she was able to go beyond her own limits with regard to the baby, how she was able to keep on giving even though she had very little left.

Being pregnant with ourselves

When a woman is pregnant nearly everything in her body undergoes a change, from her hormones to her skin, her hair and her cravings – not to mention her emotions, which seem to be on a rollercoaster. Within days mothers-to-be find themselves trapped by a network of regulations: don't smoke, don't drink, don't lift heavy items, don't do this or that. Everything is about being considerate and responsible and selfless with regard to the invisible new life inside them. And they put on weight, continually and involuntarily, and rarely only around the midriff – and for today's women self-esteem is often linked to their looks and their body. Nearly every woman has tried out a diet and more and more women have cosmetic surgery. It is mainly women who suffer from eating disorders. And all of a sudden they are pregnant, and every concern about their looks is supposed to vanish overnight. In the same way they are expected to find it perfectly easy to give up smoking and drinking, to exert restraint and to take things easy as well as to accept disadvantages in the workplace.

And then there are the partners of the pregnant women. Only very few of them are likely to have had a clue about the women's emotional life before, let alone about one on a roller-coaster. Particularly well-informed men will have heard something about premenstrual tension. Apart from that, the emotional anarchy of the other sex is probably rather alien to them. And all of a sudden those men are supposed to become fathers. For months on end nothing is even visible, let alone something that men can have feelings about. Their own bodies are the same as ever, as are their hormones. They don't suddenly have fluid retention; they don't feel sick when they see meat. Men continue to live as before – yet they are now expectant fathers.

This unequal distribution of energy culminates at childbirth. Women suffer the most incredible pains of their life; their whole bodies seem to be ripped apart by the contractions. And men watch from the sidelines like war reporters.

The birth of a child is least understood in terms of a marriage. This is exactly the moment in many relationships when a deep rift opens up between the partners. The fatal thing is that this moment is so existential, so extreme, that afterwards there is only very little awareness of this emotional abyss.

Childbirth – the start of separation

At this threshold between life and death women often feel completely abandoned. And men feel helpless at the very moment where there is actually something real to be brought to life. This is an elementary experience in human life – and only very few couples experience what they have wished for. Most women feel a deep disappointment and anger that often only surfaces much later. 'My husband kept running around nervously,' is one of the milder comments. Some men faint. Those who have always tended to run away at a crucial moment hide behind their video camera. Some men drop off with exhaustion during a prolonged birth. Some keep on asking the doctors and midwives for the latest facts and figures. Some get drunk. Some go straight from the delivery room to their lover. Others begin an affair while their wife is still in hospital.

Many women lose the respect of their husbands after child-birth, sometimes unconsciously. Even if her partner was there all the time holding her hand, a woman is likely to have felt lost and isolated. Some women are angry in a strange way, refuse to be touched by their men and ask them to leave. Childbirth reduces women to their naked physicality and forces them into complete self-awareness. All kinds of issues surface from the very depths of their emotional and physical being. They are forced to be completely passive and fully present. In such elemental abandonment we Western women quickly feel lost, cut off and angry about the ultimate truth of womanhood: having to receive and accept new life, to be exposed to an enormous power at every contraction. All we can do is open up to this life force. We can't do anything else – can't decide or change or understand anything. We can only go with the flow.

In my experience it is near enough impossible for a man to do everything right at childbirth. And in my mind hardly any woman comprehends that, by nature, during this existential creation of life, men are on the sidelines. Men don't feel what women feel. For them, everything is more or less normal. They can see that something unimaginable, painful and frightening is happening to their partners, but they cannot feel it themselves. Most of all, they can't do anything. They can only be there and try to be compassionate.

Men are used to taking action, being in control, making decisions. During childbirth they can't do anything, can't analyze, influence or even really help. After talking to a lot of men about this issue, I'd like to summarize as emphatically as I can the quintessential male experience of childbirth: helplessness, powerlessness and exclusion. I would also like to plead for more compassion from women. Women are kept conscious by their pain and are practically forced to be present in their bodies – nature has very cleverly made certain of it. But I swear, dear sisters, if we could saunter off, faint, hide behind a camera, get drunk with our mates or fall asleep in order to avoid the horrendous pain of the contractions, we would!

For many couples childbirth could become the birth of true love, because during those hours you don't meet beauty queens and brave heroes. What you meet is an elemental life force, and this expects one thing of all participants: acceptance of what is happening. Women have to go beyond themselves like never before in terms of commitment and endurance. And men have to acknowledge their unimportance as 'movers and shakers'. They have to accept being reduced to the role of a spectator, while life gives birth to itself. There is nothing to gain and to desire; it is a meeting of female pain and male powerlessness. It is a time to show deep compassion for the extreme situation of the other person. And once two people have experienced each other in this most extreme and hidden corner of their being, an unimaginable reward presents itself immediately – there is a human being where before there was none.

A new baby brings our inadequacies into the world

The first thing this little person does – after giving great happiness to its parents by simply being there – is cry. Babies are nearly always hungry. From the very first moment they are needy and demand our unconditional physical, emotional and mental presence. And nobody has told us that the animated, blissful, pure and true power of a child is one of the strongest challenges for a relationship.

Infants don't think about what they are doing. They are simply doing it. When a baby cries, its whole body cries, right down to its tiny toes. And when a baby laughs, its whole body gurgles. Children don't pretend. Children don't ask whether certain behaviour is appropriate. They are what they are. They keep on demanding whatever they need. The less we can give them, the more they will ask.

Once children have arrived, all our inadequacies become apparent. We want to give the little ones everything and find out that sometimes we haven't got much. From day one they want immediate contact and attention and for us to be occupied with them the whole time. As they always demand our whole being, all the gaps in our own hearts become apparent. Like flowers growing towards the sun, children continuously turn towards love. And if we have not received true love ourselves, we cannot give any. The flow has been interrupted. No matter how much we try to give or to compensate, we are painfully aware of our own inadequacies. Deep inside we feel guilty and withdraw behind work and other duties, or we develop into first-class leisure organizers. But children will always prefer even an imperfect but truthful life to withdrawal or a false picture-postcard family.

Of course, we only want the best for our children. And when our life isn't going that well, we try even harder. Yesterday we had a furious argument with Daddy – well, today's birthday party will be really fun. For days we've had no time for the children. Then this afternoon we *must* go swimming together. And then we realize that the noise at the birthday party is getting on our nerves and that we don't feel like making fairy cakes at all. In the pool we think of the work that needs doing and during the water fight we nearly have a panic attack.

If we really do make contact with our children, we are always aware of it immediately. Then things are easy. We giggle with them, find their stories exciting, want to go on the water slide again. In moments like that we have something to give to our children. An evening spent playing a board game with them out of duty is just a sacrifice. We might feel guilty if we don't. But deep inside our children know this very well. They have very sensitive antennae for falseness. When they sense it, they start niggling to gain attention. When they sense the emptiness of their parents' hearts, they feel utterly worthless inside.

There are two escape routes from such lifeless or laborious situations. Either you are honest with your children and say 'I don't feel like playing this game at all. I just want to curl up with a book and have some peace...' or you say 'I am really tired. I can't do the fairy cakes today – can you help me please?' or you tackle the situation with your children in all honesty and truthfulness with yourself: you acknowledge that you are absent-minded, strained, tired or numb. Once you stop using your last bit of strength to play the exemplary father or the loving mother, once you confront your inadequacies consciously, you might not experience an exciting or funny evening with your children but you might find some real closeness. Once you consciously confront your feelings, or the lack of them, amazingly enough, something begins to flow. And children sense that too. If you are aware of your inner reluctance, show your weaknesses and still say 'Oh, I'll give it a try,' then sometimes unexpected things happen.

The opposite of 'good' is 'well-meant'

A wise man used to say, 'The opposite of "good" is "well-meant".' Your empty sacrifices to your children become particularly painful when one day you expect something back from them. Now not one of the little darlings will voluntarily put the plates into the dishwasher, even though you organized perfect birthday parties for them for years. For days your youngster has answered back, been angry and not listened to a word you said, even though you've still made him cups of cocoa and tidied up after him, while secretly wanting to show him the door. You always went without because of your children. You didn't go to parties, you reluctantly abandoned your career and went to bed early every night because the little ones wouldn't go to sleep otherwise. And now you don't feel well and none of your children asks how you are without explicit prompting. Now it's your birthday and there isn't a cake or a surprise present in sight. Now your children accompany you to an important event and spend the whole time behaving like morons.

I know, the truth is bitter. But this is a harvest of empty seeds. It happens when you have sacrificed yourself, acted out a part, insisted on empty rules of behaviour. Whenever you have given because you thought you ought to, nothing of any substance has got through to your children. There is only one way to bring genuine and fulfilled human beings into this life: be true to yourself. Once you start expressing yourself to your children, complete with all your weaknesses and inadequacies, they will know who you really are. And slowly but surely you will be able to give them more energy and real fun than you ever could with all the well-meant parental role-play.

In a recent film, a cold-hearted and rigid mother tells her son, 'When I feel something for you, then it is as if I reach into a bowl with fishhooks. I can never pull out just one. They are always tangled up. That's why I'd rather leave it.'

I think that we can do no greater favour for our emotionally starved children and for our own caged hearts than bravely reach into this bowl of fishhooks.

Our children need what we find most painful

Another excursion into the realm of shadows: everybody has a stack of qualities they are unaware of. Everybody has strengths that were so strongly judged or condemned when they were growing up that they became forbidden. We all have a very comprehensive mechanism that bans such strengths completely from our thoughts, emotions and behaviour. It is our partners who remind us of them again. They often act out those repressed qualities with incredible perseverance and precision. They are sloppy, unreliable, obsessively tidy – everything that *we* find unbearable.

Even if this surfacing of our unwanted shadows is very painful, we should be grateful when they demand a place in our life again. Long ago we put heavy chains on those parts of ourselves and sent them into exile. But if we want to live a truly balanced and authentic life in the present, we need our shadows back – even if we long ago projected them onto others and now seemingly abhor them. The shadows contain important gifts and talents that we need for our development and our happiness – and sometimes for that of our children as well.

If in times of crisis, argument, separation or divorce parents weren't so focused on the polarization with their partner, they would be able to recognize that their children urgently need precisely what they cannot bear in their partner any more. It is necessary for their development. Sometimes it is even important for their survival. The tragic thing at this point of a relationship is that we are not only unaware that the shadow expressed by our partner is part of us and condemn it or hate it intensely, but we can't recognize that our children urgently need this aspect in order to remain centred. If we are always dutiful and on time, for example, our children urgently need a bit of chaos so that there is at least a little space for their playful creativity.

If, after being engaged in a power struggle with our partner for some time, we finally separate, we can't do our children a bigger favour than to really use the distance positively. Now that we have a bit of safe space, we should deal with our partner's hateful qualities and integrate them into our lives as consciously and lovingly as possible. If you found your partner's chaos unbearable, for instance, then allow yourself a bit of chaos now and again. You don't have to tell your partner. Then your children can find some peace and don't have to dissociate themselves from all those qualities that you had to dissociate yourself from as a child.

It's no use avoiding talking about your partner with your children – the important thing is what was important for us as children: the atmosphere. This matters – and children hear particularly clearly what you don't say. If you are resentful and battling for some peaceful co-existence with your partner inside yourself, then it is better to express this to your children. Only then can they look for some peace within themselves rather than send their love for both of you into separate camps.

'I don't want Daddy – I want love'

Nora showed me particularly clearly what happens to children when their parents are at war. Nora is a young woman in her early twenties. She came to me with an eating disorder that had ruled her life since her parents had separated. She had her own flat but often went to see her mother, who had remained in the former family home. She would barely have arrived before she was secretly eating everything that she could get hold of. Often she even stole money from her mother's purse. No matter whether she had just left her mother's house or her father's flat, immediately afterwards she had to buy large quantities of food and have an eating orgy in her own flat, only to vomit everything out again.

She called her state 'hanging between my parents on a rubber band'. If she was with one of them, she couldn't be with the other. There would be a sudden 'Stop' sign inside her and she wouldn't be allowed to get closer. Once she said, 'I am supposed to be able to talk to my mother since my father moved out. But it is only words. Without being prompted my mum will say that she accepts him. But really she is always angry with him, no matter what he does. The worst is when she wants to hug me. Somehow it's like touching a hot stove, she's so tense and empty. It's like starving. With my father, on the other hand, it's like choking on my own vomit. He is more relaxed than my mother, but every time I'm happy just to be with him, he starts talking about the old days, or he claims he's doing something important, or he isn't there at all.'

During our work together Nora wrote a letter to her mother which unfortunately she never sent:

You won't believe me, but I don't really care that much whether you live with Dad or the other man. Really! You think that all I want is you to get back together again. But that is not the case. What makes me so ill is your hypocrisy. You never really talk about Dad. But even so, every time you mention him it sounds as though you think he's made a mess of something again. If you nag at Dad without really talking about him then all I want is to be off. It's as if there's no place for me there. By now I really don't care whether you are with Dad or with the new man or another one or no one at all. What I don't want is your anger, your fears and your empty hugs. I am bursting. I want to vomit. I don't want to force you to go back to Dad. That's not the point. I just don't want to feel so bloody hungry and sick any more.

Nora's description is a good illustration of the fatal impact a separation can have on a child. Something always has to be sacrificed in order to keep something else. One person is there but not the other. Often one is good, because the other has to be bad. In truth there is no light without darkness – one can't exist without the other. Equally, one isn't right and the other wrong. Nora and other children still carry the memory of the true power of love inside them. Love doesn't sacrifice, love embraces, increases, shares and lets flow. Love never rules anything out.

Nora truly touched my heart. Her way of describing her feelings reminded me of one of the elemental truths: children embrace everything without knowing it. If they are forced to exclude something, then inside them something is forced to freeze or to fight for survival. Nora sometimes said, 'I love both of them – and I don't care whether they live in the same house. To me, we are all one.'

She is right. On a deep spiritual level we are all one. We are all connected to each other, whether we are geographically separated or not. Children are the expression of this connectedness. In them, two people have merged. And in them two powers form a new unit. And as long we don't accept the seemingly dark parts in our partner, then we not only freeze out love but we also cause the same thing to happen in our children.

Power struggles paralyze children

Whenever you say after a crisis or separation 'I never criticize my partner in front of the children. I don't have arguments with them in front of the children,' you are only reassuring yourself. Maybe you aren't really doing it consciously. You might not say 'Your father is an idiot' or 'I can't stand your mother's nonsense any more,' but children suffer on a more subtle level. Sentences such as 'Was watching telly all you did at Dad's?' or 'Well, your mother wants it like that' always communicate only one thing: 'The other parent is wrong.'

What wears children out is a more or less silent power struggle about attitudes and concepts. Nearly all separations involve contrasting concepts of 'videos and MacDonald's' versus 'You have to practise the piano' and 'You have to eat your greens!' One of the partners defends the territory of strict rules, high morals and political and social awareness. The other can be playful, tolerant and sloppy. The more acrimonious the separation, the more extreme the 'organic veg' vs 'fast food' battles in the family.

A recently separated woman claimed that she had found evidence of her partner's inadequacy: 'My children feel better as soon as he's gone.' Her partner, though, claims exactly the same when he is alone with the children.

Marriage is not a solution. Separation in itself is not a problem. What is important is what we think about the marriage and what we believe about the separation and our partner. If we believe that separating will traumatize our children, then our children will be traumatized. If we criticize or despise our partner when we are still living together, then our children, in their all-embracing need to love, are torn apart. If we relax as soon as soon as we have put some distance between ourselves and our partner, then our children will relax too. It is not a situation in itself that is a problem for children, but the way their parents deal with it. The most important truth here is that separation doesn't really exist. We can only really free ourselves of something by accepting it.

For that reason, if you have to separate, it is better to separate in love. The biggest favour you can do your children after a divorce is to seek forgiveness and try to understand your partner. That way your own life and that of your children will settle down again. Your own personality will develop as a result and your children will feel more grounded.

Children heal their parents

I am convinced that we are all healing links in the chain of evolution. We are on this planet to heal the story of our parents. And our children are here to heal our own story. That is emotional evolution. Year after year I can recognize in my own family how wonderfully this works. My husband and I acquired all sorts of quite different attitudes, habits and patterns from our families of origin. We both discarded a lot of them quite early on. In some ways my husband didn't fit into his family system and I didn't fit into mine. We were different, and every time we bravely stood up for ourselves and trusted our own hearts rather than acquiesced to the demands of the family, every time we went our own way successfully, something in our families of origin was healed.

Children only have to rebel against the painful and dark places in a family. I guess my fairly anxious mother nearly had a heart attack quite often during all those adventures and escapades I went through in my youth. I know that she often wanted to hold me back by threatening and sanctioning me, but today I recognize that she can find peace because I ignored so many of her fears and limitations. She can see now that many of her fears were ungrounded. She realizes that things she thought impossible really can happen. In spite of all her former anxiety, today she is proud of me and she herself is a bit freer from her own constraints because I grew beyond her without suffering any damage.

But there are all kinds of constraints, fears and pain in a family that are so elemental and deep-rooted that we are just not conscious of them. We took them on board as children and simply thought that life was like that. When I was little, for example, there was always an underlying fear of poverty. We were always scrimping, saving and shoring things up for fear of trouble in the future. At the root of it was that both my parents had suffered hunger and poverty as children. My husband, on the other hand, experienced a totally different belief system as a child. His family's principle was: 'The family must never be questioned. We have to stick together at all costs and demonstrate this to the outside world.' During the first years of our marriage we had a kind of religious war. For my husband it was unthinkable to talk about our problems with someone outside the family. If I did this, it was an utter betrayal of the whole family. And to me it was equally clear that his carefree and feckless living for the moment would ruin us.

By now you know my creed: we all urgently need from our partner whatever we find most objectionable and unimaginable. For a second time I would like to take this book as an example. Today my husband is supporting me wholeheartedly so that I can write page after page about our marriage and our family and make it known to the world. And I am working fewer hours as a therapist and trusting that we will not starve in the future.

Healing is your true legacy

As this chapter is about children, I am thinking of our daughter. Whatever my husband and I have healed already is a safe foundation for her. It is as if a little plant can grow ever better because the environment has improved – as if the sun is out more often, there are more nutrients in the soil and the quality of the water is better. So the little plant gets stronger and realizes that the world is a place of abundance and growth. That is what it is like when father and mother appreciate the differences in each other more and more and integrate them. Then a child experiences diversity and connectedness at the same time.

When our daughter was born there were many difficulties. Her birth, her entrance into this world, was strewn with obstacles. From day one she had bad colic and only found relief when we carried her around on our shoulders, rocking her around the clock. A very good friend sometimes came for an hour or two to give us a break. Then as a small child my daughter was never able to play on her own. She never slept on her own and demanded attention all the time. Sometimes it was unbearable. Sometimes all I wanted was to run away. I remember when my husband and I went on a five-day holiday for the first time and I counted the nappies that I *didn't* have to change.

Today I know how much our daughter mirrored the tension in our marriage at that time. And today I can see in my balanced, cheerful and independent daughter that the children heal together with the parents. If the parents are involved in a power struggle, there is a power struggle inside the child. If there is anxiety and tension in the family, there is anxiety and tension in the child. No matter how subtly it is expressed, if one of the partners rejects something strongly in the other, the child feels that a part of itself has been rejected.

Our daughter has many of my husband's characteristics, but she also has qualities and talents of mine. In the same way that my husband and I have grown closer together over the years and can accept and appreciate each other's qualities more, so the different polarities in our daughter have connected. Over time she has become calmer and doesn't dither as much, and there are fewer absolute issues with her. She can also surf between my husband and me much more easily and tap into whichever resource she needs at any given moment. In quite an obvious way she knows to do maths with Daddy and writing with Mum. But on a deeper level, too, she knows that she has various resources at her disposal. Recently she told a friend: 'My dad is the one to be silly with, and with my mum I can talk to the angels.' As for fast food, Dad is the first port of call, whereas if she wants to sleep over with a friend for the third night running, she sees to it that she gets Mum on her own before she asks for permission.

This wealth of possibility gives space for a child's personality to develop fully. But true stability, in my mind, doesn't come through diversity but through the acceptance and valuing of their own individuality. I can't say it often enough – children are love, and in order to be themselves they want to love. On a deeply unconscious level they are only allowed to love what their parents love. Their own love is not allowed to transcend the love of their parents. That is the price that all children pay in order to remain within their families.

For me, our daughter is a soul of her own born into our family. We cannot really educate her or give her anything beyond learning to love and to accept more and more aspects of other people and of the world. But this probably makes her, too, feel valued as we come close to the true nature and the depth of her soul.

I am sure our daughter, with her wonderfully witty and strong nature, has been born for a good reason. Her soul, too, is embarking on an adventure and in the course of her life she will heal a lot in her father and her mother – far beyond what we are able to accept from each other today, far beyond what I can even imagine...

Abortion – a time for grief

The last paragraph would have been a good ending to this chapter, but I can't exclude another aspect of having children: abortion. So far I have tried to describe what an enormous revolution it is for a relationship when a child is born. And I have mentioned how many relationships don't survive this revolution intact. Sometimes mothers and fathers fear the massive power and the changes a baby would bring into their life so much that they don't want the child to be born. There are numerous reasons against children: the relationship not being strong enough, the possible disability of the child, the fear of responsibility, the circumstances or the job situation... I have heard many a reason and in all cases have learned something baffling – even in the case of a very early termination, it is always about a child. What I am saying is that a termination is not simply a quick medical intervention removing a cluster of cells. Every time a person dies. And when a person dies, it is in our nature to say goodbye to them and to grieve appropriately.

I am saying this regardless of any church dogma or religious morals. My view is based on my experience with clients. For me, abortion has always been a helpful option provided by modern medicine for an emergency. I have never had the slightest unease about it for a good reason – my IU device slipped and I became pregnant by a man I didn't know very well. Then one night, when I was alone in bed, I experienced a sense of connection that I had never felt before. I woke up with the feeling that there was somebody inside me. Of course I thought, 'That's stupid!' But I couldn't get back to sleep because the feeling was so intense. Then came the sudden thought: 'I'm pregnant!' And again: 'That's rubbish! You have the IU thing, and your period isn't really late.' Yet, after a second night with equally strange sensations I went and bought a pregnancy test. It was positive! I went to my gynaecologist. She confirmed it. Now came the question: 'Shall I have a termination?' If my friends had ever asked me, I would always have said, 'Yes.' And now everything inside me was shouting, 'No!' After half an hour of pros and cons I was absolutely clear, from the roots of my hair to the soles of my feet: I would bring this child into the world regardless.

I thought this experience, this unambiguousness, was a personal exception, my own individual inexplicable emotional truth. I didn't draw any conclusions about the pros and cons of termination per se. Since then, during my years as a therapist I have learned that apart from the birth of a child, the major reason for a relationship being poisoned and destroyed is a termination. Most women are surprised when they discover that it was this event that brought about the death of something in their relationship.

One couple made the issue particularly poignant. The man had urged the woman to have an abortion and during our work he repeatedly talked about 'the abortion', while she talked of 'our Clare' and wept with grief, even though it had happened six years ago and the two had had another child since. Working with this couple, I understood more clearly than ever before that at the moment of conception a soul appears between a couple. In this case it was 'Clare'. The two people concerned had never talked about the episode, but their sex life had dried up. The healing process that unfolded during our sessions was very painful but very clear: all it needed was some mourning and acceptance of this soul. When the mother was allowed to express her grief and the father was finally able to say 'our daughter', peace and closeness suddenly surfaced between them again. One day the man finally said, crying, 'My Clare.' Then the woman stopped crying and order was restored within the family.

I have found that with nearly all abortions it is important to appreciate the soul that has come and gone, to say goodbye to it and to mourn it sufficiently. With modern people and high-tech medicine this is not always an easy process. But in all the cases I know of, when a termination was carried out in the belief that it was simply a cluster of cells that was removed, something died within the woman or the relationship until the soul could be mourned. Sometimes women have told me with embarrassment that after a termination they have had the feeling that the child has lived on. If they are still with the same partner, they often feel as if the child is standing between them.

To state it clearly one more time: I am not against abortion for moral, ethical or dogmatic reasons. I believe there are situations in the lives of mothers and fathers that more than justify an abortion.

Only I have learned that we have to take that step consciously. We have to appreciate the being and say goodbye to it.

This chapter is called 'Children of love'. By nature, children find their way into this world because two people conjoin physically for a moment. In most cases, therefore, children emerge from an ecstatic connection of two people linked by their hearts. Of all the attempts to describe this amazing, unique process of creating life, Kahlil Gibran's words have always moved me the most:

> *Your children are not your children.*
> *They are the sons and daughters of life's longing for itself,*
> *For they have their own thoughts.*
> *They come through you but not from you,*
> *And though they are with you yet they belong not to you.*
> *You may give them your love but not your thoughts,*
> *For they have their own thoughts.*
> *You must house their bodies but not their souls,*
> *For their souls dwell in the house of tomorrow, which you*
> *cannot visit, not even in your dreams.*
> *You may strive to be like them, but seek not to make them*
> *like you.*
> *For life does not go backward nor tarries with yesterday.*[7]

7. Kahlil Gibran, *The Prophet*, Arkana, London, 1992, p.22

15

Love is ... work, diligence, discipline and reward

Exciting and loving relationships demand a lot from us. The deeper, stronger and more intimate they are, the less space there is to deceive ourselves. A relationship challenges us to recognize that we aren't everything we believe ourselves to be when we are on our own. It challenges us time and again to strip off, to be naked in our innermost core – the place where we are love.

We can only experience this deepest of all spiritual truths in relationships with other people when we are truly committed to ourselves. Otherwise we can read up on our divine nature, we can meditate about it and study it, but it won't do us any good. I know a lot of people with a truly inspiring theoretical knowledge and a vast spiritual library. But many of them seem like seductive virgins – as yet unkissed.

In reality, the amount of vitality and fulfilment in our life is solely dependent on how much we experience our inner truth. How much we experience ourselves as loving beings. How much we trust, challenge and transcend our own selves to bring this truth into being – with patience, perseverance, courage and discipline. How much we dare to follow our hearts and present ourselves as vulnerable. Most of all, how much we can avoid judging our partner and how much we can forgive them. If we feel lonely, cold and empty in our relationship or in our life, then there is a simple path back towards warmth: we have to find a focal point for our love – what it is doesn't really matter – and let our attention, gratitude, forgiveness and affection flow consciously towards it.

Give it a try. Think of someone, whoever comes to your mind, and open your heart. Maybe you remember a particularly good time with someone and want to thank them. Maybe you are brave and decide to forgive an old issue that locks you in resentment with someone. Maybe you decide to really go for it and unleash all your compassion on your partner, even though you are in the middle of a long-running argument.

Just close your eyes and take a few deep breaths. Be aware that your breath is flowing in through your chest and moving deep down into your pelvic region. Give your full attention to your breath and relax with a sigh or by yawning with your whole body. Look for a connecting thought and focus on the middle of your chest. Do you feel something opening up there? While you are indulging in this feeling of wellbeing, notice warmth spreading through you. Something begins to flow inside you and you feel softer inside. You feel the love inside yourself. You sense your divine core.

Overnight superstars

Stop waiting and longing for a Mr or Ms Perfect, worthy of your love, who will just drop by eventually. Stop being angry and vengeful when others aren't perfect or behave in an unpleasant way. Don't wait until everything is right before you say 'Yes, let's move in together/marry/have a baby.' Instead, simply decide as often as you can to look for the loveable heart of the people you meet and direct your love to them. This love is God's gift – and yet it is *your* conscious decision. Every day, every hour, every minute, you can consciously decide to either love or not love.

If you do decide to unfold the love in your life, then you need perseverance and discipline. Most people don't want to know about that. We are all so used to simply consuming. We are looking for a drive-in and a microwave for our needs. And we see superstars who apparently appear overnight. They seem to be like packet soup – just a cupful of hot water and hey presto, they're ready! In reality, all those great sportspeople, artists, actors or scientists have extraordinary talents, just as everybody else boasts extraordinary inner love. People who achieve truly great things commit themselves to their passion, devote themselves to their dream and train and practise far beyond their limits. They cope with numerous defeats and setbacks and usually make a great many sacrifices in order to reach their goals.

The truth is that we cannot achieve anything important in our lives without perseverance and discipline. With just a little bit of discipline we can initiate something. With total perseverance and discipline we can change a whole life. Total perseverance and discipline mean loving fully the whole time. That's a championship title worth striving for. It may sound difficult, but the truth is that life is not meant to be easy. From an emotional point of view, we come here to heal, to learn and to contribute. Our soul doesn't care whether we are enjoying it or not. Its aim is healing, personal development and the transformation of old wounds.

Do your homework – otherwise it does you

It was Chuck Spezzano who gave me this wonderful piece of wisdom: 'Do your homework – otherwise it does you.' What did he mean? If we are alert, persevering and disciplined, always ready to continue developing, if we open up our minds and hearts to others and to new things, if we are prepared to take on leadership and to bear the consequences of everything that we cause, if we are willing to stand by our own truth, then we do our homework. If not, then fate, problems, 'wrong' partners, illness and life itself will see to our development, only apparently against our will.

Life is an eternal sequence of opportunities for growth that we normally call problems. Most people don't want to know this either. Fear of the pain the problems might cause means most people try to avoid them, ignore them or repress them. But time and again we are challenged to face them and to solve them – particularly if we try to avoid them. It is this process that gives life its true meaning. This is real evolution. We can only grow if there is some resistance, because this challenges our strengths, our potential and our faith. And problems cause pain – until we are prepared to face them head on, look at them and accept them with all our curiosity, commitment, understanding and love. Only then will the pain end and life gain some lightness – until the next so-called 'problem', the next task to be met with perseverance and discipline. And so on until the next reward.

Don't wait until you can say: 'We've finally made it!' That is the wrong approach to a relationship, as is: 'First I have to find Mr/Ms Right...' A long-term relationship is like crafting stone. First you hack away the lumpy bits with a hammer and a chisel. In the later stages the tools become more delicate and the workings incredibly fine. Every day your partner does something differently from how you would do it. That means that every day there is something you can learn from your partner. When you first try out this approach you will probably have to hack away quite big chunks. Maybe your partner is cheating on you or is inconsiderate. It's not easy hacking away at those lumps in the hope of creating an aesthetically pleasing shape eventually. I know that it works. But time and again you will need willpower to heal your relationship, to fully commit yourself to your partner, to express your whole truth, to look at the lovelessness inside yourself and to acknowledge your own lack of commitment.

Love out of a crisis

There is one final question: 'Is it really worth the bother?' You know my answer: '*Yesssssssssssssssssssssssssss!*' A crisis is a source of energy. A crisis gives birth to love. A crisis is an opportunity. A weathered crisis always leaves traces behind: more confidence, courage, intimacy, vitality. We must stop doubting. We know that we can make it. And while battling through all the challenges and storms of a relationship, it becomes more intense and we both grow.

You can recognize people who have been on such a journey: they give off more calmness and joyfulness. They know that life is full of opportunities for growth and they face them patiently. Often they smile when they remember back to how they once thought that a crisis was a problem and that they wanted to run away from it.

The big challenge in a relationship is how we can experience freedom and love, depth and light-heartedness at the same time. How can we accept and acknowledge that the other person is different while still keeping our emotional intimacy and even deepening it? A while ago I talked to a couple bursting with such questions and searching for the next step in their relationship. Both were surprised during our talks to discover that deep inside they held the firm belief that they should never wholly commit themselves to another person, never truly abandon themselves to love because the other person might die. This conclusion baffled me very much and my first instinctive thought was: 'How fulfilling it would be, if my husband died, to be able to mourn so much love!'

People are more afraid of love than of anything else. We would rather die than take the risk of truly living and loving. I think that these days we have come to a watershed. The old systems aren't functioning any more. Once whole lives were geared towards 'higher, faster, further, bigger'. But the foundation of that system is fear – fear of not being good enough, fear of not possessing enough. In this system relationships are seen through a filter of competitiveness. 'Do I get enough attention and care? Does my partner get more than me? If I invest too much, will I be losing too much?' The driving force behind a lot of our behaviour is a deep-seated feeling of worthlessness. We feel inadequate and have a fear of loss. We constantly feel that we are not good enough. So we have to make more of an effort to achieve, to create, to achieve even more, to do even more and to make more of an effort...

Day by day we achieve even more even faster. But we don't feel satisfied. Quite the opposite – for more and more people life feels like standing in a swamp and sinking deeper with every step they try to take. Confusing winning with success has led our Western world into a dead-end street. From childhood onwards we have learned to win and now we are standing here with the trophies – in a traffic jam. And fewer and fewer people are applauding us because every one of our victories creates more losers. As soon as we win, someone else loses. And in global terms, this winner-loser game automatically drives us into a corner. Social systems, businesses, families, relationships and individuals are paralyzed or collapse.

No winners without losers

In my view our current worldwide crisis is our greatest opportunity for evolution. We have to acknowledge that we are all in relationships – with everybody and everything. And at the moment there are no victories per se. There are only triumphs that make others losers. That is why it is vital for everybody to learn how to be successful. Success means making the best of ourselves. Success means the best for me is also the best for others. Success means everybody works together. We all learn to have new kinds of relationships. Everybody – men as well as women – discovers the nurturing principle of mothering in themselves. We all become a catalyst for success in the people we encounter. Once other people's lives – and the world itself – change for the better because of what we do, we will automatically feel successful and fulfilled.

True success happens when we devote our life to personal healing and development, as I have described in this book. For that we don't have to go into a retreat, nor do we need therapy. All we have to do is to look around us – at our families, our work, our friends. If our life seems threatened, unsafe, lifeless, frozen or lonely, we should stop looking for scapegoats. Our questions should rather be: 'What do I have to give that I haven't given before? When do I act out of a false sense of duty? When do I only give out of politeness and fear of rejection? When do I give only in order to be recognized?' This kind of giving will drain you. It creates the feeling of never getting enough. We can only truly give when we are prepared to receive only what is best for ourselves. In order to truly give we have to value ourselves first.

I have noticed that most people are afraid to live their own greatness. We shrink to the smallest common denominator so that we can fit in and belong. We make sure that nobody can criticize us, that we don't hurt anybody, that we are never different from those whose consent and attention we crave. Or we become self-righteous and claim to be revolutionaries. We debate political issues, we discuss the war in Iraq, the pros and cons of amalgam fillings, state pensions and eating beef. We become successful and make decisions about the closing down of subsidiaries in faraway countries. We can't deal with the pettiness of our friends and don't invite them to dinner any more, but greet them in passing with an overly friendly smile. But this apparently brave willingness to argue doesn't give us what we are looking for either.

Say 'yes'!

True success will flow into your life once you express yourself, once you acknowledge what you want and once you live out your true life tasks. Have you been wanting to speak out for a long time? Have you been dreaming of a different job? Have you been passionate about starting a project? Are you still clinging to security, not daring to finally let go of all your meaningless duties and joyless routines? Are you are hiding behind doubts, mediocrity, tradition and comfort? Are you saying 'I should ... I ought to ... if only ... soon...'?

Everything would change if only you were willing to look at yourself in all honesty. If you were prepared to show your own truths and express them. If you learned to stop repressing your pain and accepted it. If you began to forgive yourself and others for your apparent mistakes. If you were willing to give up judgement and criticism. If you were ready to opt out of safe but lifeless routines. If you were prepared to take risks again. If you were willing to listen to your inner voice or other people's guidance. If you were prepared to stand up for another person or issue. Then you would finally discover your talents, your unused strengths, your creativity, your purpose in life. Then all the gifts and emotional tasks you have brought into this life would unfold all of a sudden. When this happens it is as if the former reluctance, the blockages, the pain, the hopelessness and the obstacles in your life suddenly form part of a bigger picture and make sense. And all of a sudden your life makes a difference.

We all have to find purpose and meaning in our life in order to be fulfilled and happy. Then we can help others to do the same. Together we can redeem the world. If you take one step forward, if you heal your own life, then everybody else around you is also able to take one step forward. The further you proceed with your development, the better others around you will feel. Once you are happier, more successful and alive, then everybody in contact with you will feel the strength you are radiating, consciously and unconsciously.

The turbo-chargers on this path are intimate relationships. In no other situation can we get to know ourselves more quickly and more precisely. Everywhere we fall short of our ideal will be apparent in a relationship with another person. And the closer we get to ourselves, the more profound the opportunities for self-knowledge – and the more profound the insights into everything that we have kept hidden from ourselves and would never have looked at otherwise. As unpleasant as they might sometimes feel, intimate relationships are the royal road to transforming your life. Each painful lesson challenges us to move forward, but once learned, it immediately leads to greater intimacy and confidence.

One of the biggest steps you can take is to truly commit to another person – to say: 'I will share my path with you – the bad times as well as the good times. I will entrust myself to you, even when things get difficult. You are my mirror. In your healing, your happiness, your fulfilment, I recognize my own healing and my power to heal others.' The very biggest step forward, your greatest gift to the world, though, is the one you take when you love yourself.

A friend shaken up by a recent marital crisis told me he had met a very remarkable woman. They were both part of a small group of friends that was talking very openly about having affairs. There were a few confessions and the sad and resigned consensus was that these days affairs were likely to be part of nearly every long-term relationship. Eventually this remarkable woman had turned the conversation around abruptly by saying, 'I can't say anything about affairs. I have been married for 13 years and have other priorities.' The friends looked at her in confusion and doubt. Was she kidding? Had she simply shut out the facts of modern-day life? But the remarkable woman explained that before her marriage she had lived quite a wild life and at one point even had three relationships going at the same time. Then she had met her husband and one day had decided to share her life with him. They had got married and had said, 'I do.' From that day on she had considered that sentence her life task. It was her commitment to marriage.

AFTERWORD
You can make it on your own, but two's company

Only very few people have trodden this path of believing, loving, forgiving and healing. I have written this book to communicate hope and knowledge and to show by the example of my own life that miracles are possible when taking it. I also know that only reading this book once will rarely give you more than a vague idea of what is possible. In order to find true and fulfilling love you need patience and perseverance. That's why I am asking you to read this book again and again. There will be times in your life when everything seems to be hopeless. Sometimes there will be setbacks. Sometimes you will be full of anger and hatred. Sometimes you will be absolutely sure that everything is your partner's fault. Sometimes all you will want to do is separate.

That's why a book like this has to be read more often. Read the parts that are important to you as often as you can so that you are reminded that there is an alternative, that there is love in the other person, that carrying on does make sense. With every reading, especially if you leave gaps in between, you will gain new insights. If an insight moves you deeply, talk about it. Talk to your partner. Talk in particular about your feelings. Read the parts that are important to you aloud to your partner. Ask them to read this book too – or at least the important bits.

Don't try to make excuses. In order to transform a relationship, initially it is sufficient for one of you to make a firm decision to move forward. This person will develop so much love and strength that on a deep level the other one will be touched and somehow changed too. But be careful! I know people who have got lost on this path – people who suddenly became too enlightened for the rest of the world. Every catharsis brings with it the danger, especially for women, of making increasing demands on their partners. 'I have come this far but my husband doesn't want to develop with me. He doesn't understand what it is all about. He is cynical about it, judgemental and unconsciously craving for acceptance. How can I stay with someone like that? How can I transform the relationship...?'

This kind of approach manoeuvres you into a trap. When you move forward in your personal development there's no gold medal for achievement, only the challenge of finding new levels of compassion and forgiveness. Maybe you are now able to express your own truth more bravely. Maybe you have undergone a painful process that has brought you closer to yourself. Maybe your partner and the people around you haven't come this far. Maybe they are all still trying to hide behind their respective roles. Maybe they still have secrets and condemn others. All that should not rob you of your peace of mind. The others don't need new demands or condemnations from you, but new understanding and fresh compassion. They need somebody whose help they can accept.

Of course all this is easier when two people commit to each other. Of course it would be ideal if both you and your partner read this book. If initially your partner isn't willing, that shouldn't be an excuse for you to stop. Don't forget, they are only your mirror. Something important for your own healing is equally locked and uncommunicative inside you, and you are just as unconscious of it as your partner is of the facets that you recognize so clearly. Maybe you are reading all this eagerly but you lack the strength to act accordingly. Maybe on an unconscious level you don't really want to share the book with your partner but are only seeking ammunition in your ongoing war. Remember, on a deeper level, your partner will notice immediately whether they are truly invited into a new kind of relationship or not.

The most important thing is not to give up, no matter how difficult things get and how often you seem to fail. If you take on board all the messages contained in this book, then things can feel even worse in the beginning. When the love inside us is pushing its way out into freedom, sometimes it can seem as if we are losing control over our lives. In such moments take the book and read it, so that your mind can calm down. Love needs another opportunity to work inside you. For that, you have to tame your judgemental, suspicious mind. You have to unlearn a lot, shed old habits and practise new things repeatedly until they are processed sufficiently and can sink into the foundations of your consciousness. There they can germinate, like new seeds, in order to blossom at the right time.

It is not easy in these confused and ignorant times to rediscover and liberate all the love that is buried inside us. But if you invest true courage and honesty in the process and seek the path to love and fulfilment with all your heart, then life will surely lead you onto that path. Take note of where the answers to your innermost questions come from. Trust what heals and helps you and not what others find healing and helpful. God rarely looks like an old man with a grey beard. And when we meet love, it rarely has wings.

In whatever form help appears, we have to make the decision to receive it. In the end it is always down to us to make peace with the world as it is. In the end it is not about finding a suitable partner, it is about reconquering life for ourselves. Nobody else can do this for us. But if we ask for it, all the powers in Heaven and Earth will support us in this greatest of all tasks.

Further Reading

Coelho, Paulo: *Eleven Minutes*. London: HarperCollins, 2004

Katie, Byron, and Mitchell, Stephen: *Loving What Is: How Four Questions Can Change Your Life*, London: Rider & Co., 2002

Leider, Richard J., and Shapiro, David A.: *Repacking Your Bags: Lighten Your Load for the Rest of Your Life*, Maidenhead: McGraw Hill, 2000

Long, Barry: *Making Love: Sexual Love the Divine Way*, London: Barry Long Books, 1998

Pierrakos, Eva, and Saly, Judith: *Creating Union: The Pathwork of Relationship*, Charlottesville, Virginia: Pathwork Press, 1997

Richardson, Diana: *The Love Keys: The Art of Ecstatic Sex – A Unique Guide to Love and Sexual Fulfilment*, London: HarperCollins, 1999

Spezzano, Dr Chuck: *Wholeheartedness: Healing Our Heartbreaks*, London: Hodder Mobius, 2000

Spezzano, Dr Chuck: *Getting Along with Absolutely Anyone: 50 Ways to Make Every Relationship Work*, London: Hodder Mobius, 2001

Tolle, Eckhart, and Allen, Marc: *Practicing the Power of Now: Meditations and Exercises and Core Teachings for Living the Liberated Life*, Novato, California: New World Library, 2001

Walsch, Neale Donald: *Conversations with God. An Uncommon Dialogue*, London: Hodder Mobius, 1997

Wapnick, Kenneth: *The 50 Miracle Principles of a Course in Miracles*, Lithia Springs, Georgia: New Leaf Distribution Company, 1994

Titles of Related Interest

Dawn Breslin's Power Book by Dawn Breslin
Dr Lucy Atcheson's Guide to Perfect Relationships by Dr Lucy Atcheson
Everything I've Ever Learned About Love by Lesley Garner
Inspiration by Dr Wayne W. Dyer
The Law of Attraction by Esther and Jerry Hicks
You Can Have What You Want by Michael Neill
You Can Heal Your Life by Louise L. Hay

We hope you enjoyed this Hay House book.
If you would like to receive a free catalogue featuring additional
Hay House books and products, or if you would like information
about the Hay Foundation, please contact:

Hay House UK Ltd
292B Kensal Rd • London W10 5BE
Tel: (44) 20 8962 1230; Fax: (44) 20 8962 1239
www.hayhouse.co.uk

***

Published and distributed in the United States of America by:
Hay House, Inc. • PO Box 5100 • Carlsbad, CA 92018-5100
Tel: (1) 760 431 7695 or (800) 654 5126;
Fax: (1) 760 431 6948 or (800) 650 5115
www.hayhouse.com

Published and distributed in Australia by:
Hay House Australia Ltd • 18/36 Ralph St • Alexandria NSW 2015
Tel: (61) 2 9669 4299; Fax: (61) 2 9669 4144
www.hayhouse.com.au

Published and distributed in the Republic of South Africa by:
Hay House SA (Pty) Ltd • PO Box 990 • Witkoppen 2068
Tel/Fax: (27) 11 706 6612 • orders@psdprom.co.za

Distributed in Canada by:
Raincoast • 9050 Shaughnessy St • Vancouver, BC V6P 6E5
Tel: (1) 604 323 7100; Fax: (1) 604 323 2600

***

Sign up via the Hay House UK website to receive the Hay House
online newsletter and stay informed about what's going on with
your favourite authors. You'll receive bimonthly announcements
about discounts and offers, special events, product highlights,
free excerpts, giveaways, and more!
www.hayhouse.co.uk